Contemporary Theory Workbook

book 2

by Margaret Brandman

Exclusive distributors for Australia and New Zealand
Encore Music Distributors
227 Napier St, Fitzroy VIC 3065 Australia
Phone +61 3 9415 6677
Facsimile +61 3 9415 6655
Email sales@encoremusic.com.au

This book © Copyright 2017 by Margaret Brandman trading as Jazzem Music
46 Gerrale St, Cronulla NSW 2230 Australia
ISBN 978-0-949683-44-1
ORDER NUMBER MMP 8068
International copyright secured (APRA/AMCOS). All rights reserved.

Unauthorised reproduction of any part of this publication by any means,
including photocopying, is an infringement of copyright.

Contents - Part A

Introduction 4
Lesson 1 Note-naming on Leger Lines 5
Lesson 2 Simple and Compound Intervals. 9th and 10th 6
Lesson 3 Note-naming exercises using Compound Intervals and
             Leger Line notes 7
Lesson 4 The Demisemiquaver or 32nd Note 8
Lesson 5 Relative Minor Scales. Part A - The Natural Minor Scale 9
Lesson 6 Relative Minor Scales. Part B - The Harmonic Minor Scale ... 10
Lesson 7 More on the Harmonic Minor Scale 11
Lesson 8 Relative Minor Scales. Part C - The Melodic Minor Scale 12
Lesson 9 The Full Cycle of Fifths including Minor Keys 13
Lesson 10 How to assess the Key of a Melody 14
Lesson 11 Tonic Minor Scales 15
Lesson 12 More Repeat Signs and associated terms 16
Lesson 13 Transposition 17
Lesson 14 Minor Scale and Transposition Review 18
Lesson 15 Simple Meter Time-Signatures 19
Lesson 16 Compound Meter Time-Signatures 20
Lesson 17 More on Compound Meter Time-Signatures 21
Lesson 18 The Triplet 22
Lesson 19 The Duplet 23
Lesson 20 Review of Time-Signatures, Triplets and Duplets 24
Lesson 21 Modulation 25
Lesson 22 More on Modulation 26
Lesson 23 Interval Qualities: Perfect and Major 27
Lesson 24 Interval Qualities: Minor 28
Lesson 25 Interval Qualities: Diminished 29
Lesson 26 Interval Qualities: Augmented 30
Lesson 27 Inversion of Intervals 31
Lesson 28 Interval Sounds 32
Lesson 29 Uneven or Odd Time-Signatures 33
Lesson 30 Review of Triads 34
Lesson 31 Major 7th, Dominant 7th and Major 6th Chords 35
Lesson 32 Minor 7th and Minor 6th Chords 36
Lesson 33 Diminished 7th and Half-Diminished 7th Chords 37
Lesson 34 Chord Review Exercises 38
Lesson 35 Test Your Knowledge 39
Answer Sheet 40

Contents - Part B

Lesson 1	The Modes	43
Lesson 2	Modal Sounds	44
Lesson 3	The Dorian Mode	45
Lesson 4	The Phrygian Mode	46
Lesson 5	The Lydian Mode	47
Lesson 6	The Mixolydian Mode	48
Lesson 7	The Aeolian Mode	49
Lesson 8	The Locrian Mode	50
Lesson 9	Modes in Review	51
Lesson 10	Single, Double and Triple Dotted Notes	52
Lesson 11	Syncopation	53
Lesson 12	Triad Review and Triads found in Major Keys	54
Lesson 13	The Major Chord-Table	55
Lesson 14	Triads found in Minor Keys	56
Lesson 15	The Minor Chord-Table	57
Lesson 16	Figuring	58
Lesson 17	Exercises on Chord-Tables and Figuring	59
Lesson 18	The Two Smallest Note Values - 64th notes, 128th notes	60
Lesson 19	Rarer Notes and Rests	61
Lesson 20	The Pentatonic Scale	62
Lesson 21	The Blues Scale	63
Lesson 22	Swing Timing	64
Lesson 23	The Whole-Tone Scale	65
Lesson 24	The Diminished Scale	66
Lesson 25	Comparing the Simple and Compound Time Signatures	67
Lesson 26	Naming Intervals within a line of music	68
Lesson 27	Inversions of Compound Intervals	69
Lesson 28	Introduction to Harmony - Perfect and Plagal Cadences	70
Lesson 29	The use of Secondary Chords and the Imperfect Cadence	71
Lesson 30	The Interrupted or Surprise Cadence	72
Lesson 31	Exercises on Chord Progressions and Cadences	73
Lesson 32	Acoustics	74
Lesson 33	Ornaments	75
Lesson 34	More Ornaments	76
Lesson 35	Test Your Knowledge	77
Answer Sheet		78

Introduction

These books are a part of my Contemporary series of books and ear-training materials. The Contemporary series provides an holistic view of music covering the practical, theoretical and aural aspects of music.

Taking a practical and common sense approach, the Contemporary Theory Workbooks provide students with an overview of many aspects of music theory, revealing many musical mysteries which other traditional books neglected in the past. The information presented allows the student to venture into popular, jazz and contemporary idioms as well as providing a solid foundation in music of the western classic tradition. The page-per-lesson format encourages the student to see the whole picture (gestalt) of each topic in a much reduced time frame.

There is emphasis on the interval approach to assist with the comprehension of many concepts and to foster music speed reading and learning in any clef.

In this book all types of minor scales plus other scales including modes are approached from both written and keyboard pattern points of view. The Cycle of Fifths extending to minor keys and the standard four-note chords are also covered in these books. These tools are invaluable for the improvising musician as well as the reader.

To simplify the topic of rhythm and duration, spatial diagrams have been presented. By colouring them in using the colour system presented in the Contemporary Piano Method Book 2A, students will be able to fully understand the duration of notes through the accelerated learning tools of touch, spatial orientation and colour.

Use of the colour as a memory aid will promote the understanding of time signatures. Students are advised to highlight the lower number of any time-signature using the Contemporary series standard colour for the note value. Refer to the lessons on time signatures, for instance Lesson 20 in Part A of Book 1, Lessons 19 - 22 in Part B of Book 1, and Lessons 15 -19 in Part A of Book 2.

The Contemporary series colours are as follows:
- * double whole note/breve .... mauve
- * whole note/semibreve ....purple
- * half note/minim .... yellow
- * quarter note/crotchet .... blue
- * eighth note/quaver.............................red
- * sixteenth note/ semiquaver .... green
- * thirty-second note/demisemiquaver ....brown

Other materials in the Contemporary series to use alongside this book are:

1) *Contemporary Chord Workbook* (Book 1) This is the ideal companion to Book 2 of the Contemporary Theory Workbooks and may be completed in tandem to consolidate and amplify the area of chords and harmony for both classical and modern pieces.

2) *Contemporary Aural Course* (Set Two onwards) Helping students understand the sounds and language of music, through listening, singing and transcription.

3) *Contemporary Piano Method* - Books 2A, 2B, 3 and 4.

I trust you will find this series an enjoyable and interesting way to learn about the musical language.

Margaret Brandman. (Dr)
Ph.D. (Mus. Arts), B.Mus (Syd),
T.Mus.A., A.Mus.A., ASA T. Dip

LESSON ONE

NOTE-NAMING ON LEGER LINES

By using the interval method learned in Book One of this series, note-naming on Leger Lines can be approached in the same way as note-naming on the staff.

Find a Signpost 'C' and work by intervals from this starting note. On the Great Staff, the signpost notes to use would be **Very High C**, **Very Low C** and **Middle C.**

Intervals

S (same) = Prime
St (step) = Second
Sk (skip) = Third
Sk +1 (skip-plus-one) = Fourth
J (jump) = Fifth
6th = Sixth
7th = Seventh
8ve = Octave or Eighth

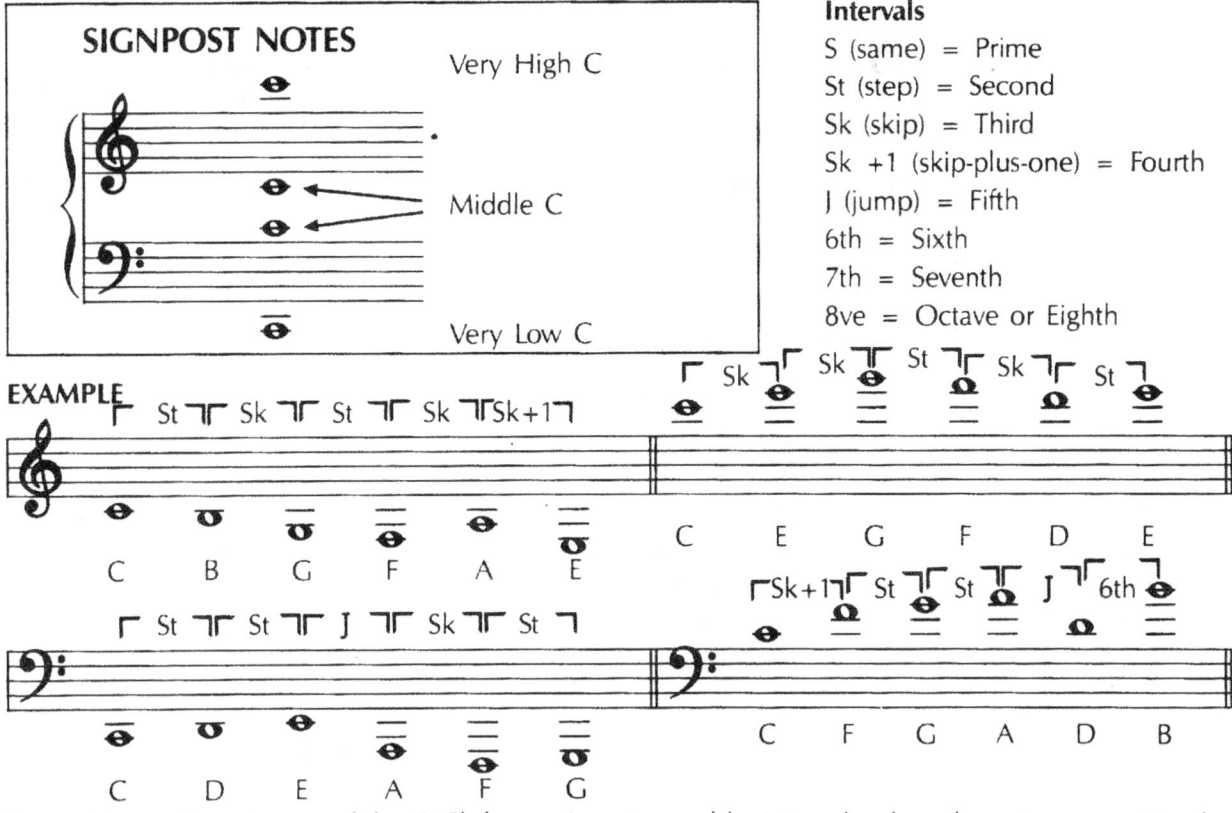

To read Leger Lines in any of the C Clefs, continue to read by intervals when the notes move into the Leger Lines above and below the staff.

EXERCISE

Name these Leger Line notes in the various clefs. Begin each exercise by writing in a Signpost C to work from. If you need to, write an alphabetical list of note names on scrap paper, to work from.

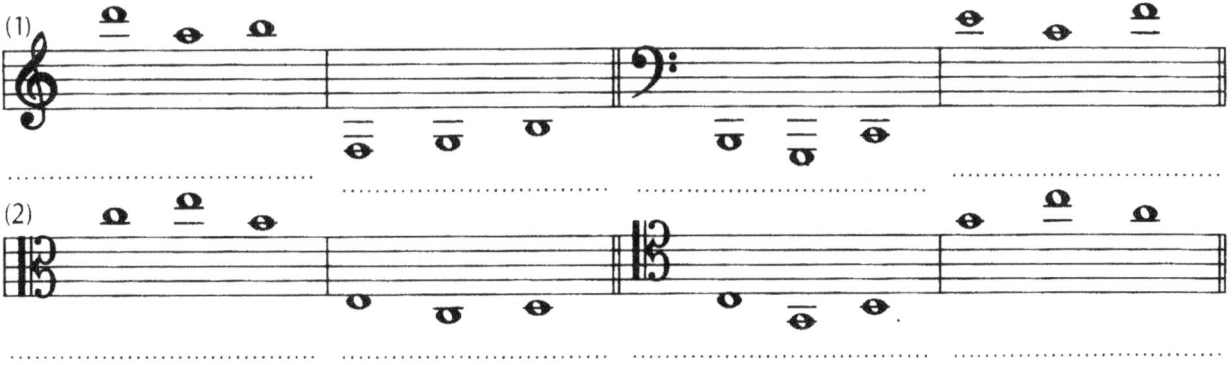

5

LESSON TWO

SIMPLE AND COMPOUND INTERVALS

A SIMPLE INTERVAL is an interval which is an Octave or less in size.
The Simple Intervals are: Prime (1st), 2nd, 3rd, 4th, 5th, 6th, 7th & 8ve.

A COMPOUND INTERVAL is one that is larger than an Octave.
For Instance: 9th, 10th, 11th, 12th, 13th, 14th and 15th.
The Fifteenth is the Double Octave.

COMPOUND INTERVALS CAN BE NAMED IN TWO WAYS

The names of the notes in the interval of a Ninth are the same as those in the interval of a Second, the only difference being that the Ninth is an Octave further away from the Second.

Similarly the interval of a Tenth uses the same notes as the Third, the Eleventh is the same as the Fourth and so on.

To find out what the larger interval is the same as, deduct '7' from the larger number. e.g. the 13th is the same as the 6th; 13 - 7 = 6.

Therefore the two ways to name each interval are:

1. As a Compound Interval   2 As the larger number

A Compound Second	=	A Ninth
A Compound Third	=	A Tenth
A Compound Fourth	=	An Eleventh
A Compound Fifth	=	A Twelfth
A Compound Sixth	=	A Thirteenth
A Compound Seventh	=	A Fourteenth
A Compound Eighth	=	A Fifteenth

In this book we will be using two of these intervals, the NINTH and the TENTH.

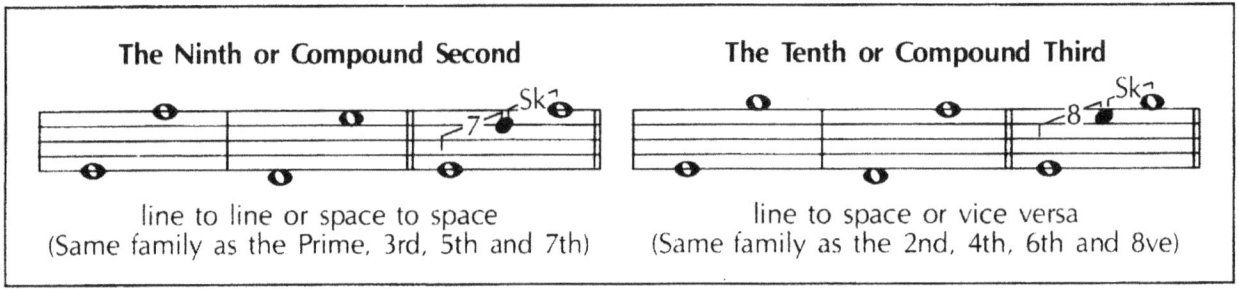

The Ninth or Compound Second
line to line or space to space
(Same family as the Prime, 3rd, 5th and 7th)

The Tenth or Compound Third
line to space or vice versa
(Same family as the 2nd, 4th, 6th and 8ve)

◆◆◆◆◆◆◆◆◆◆◆◆◆◆◆◆◆◆◆◆◆◆◆◆◆◆◆◆◆◆◆

EXERCISES

(1) Name these intervals in two ways; as Compound Seconds and Thirds and as Ninths and Tenths. (Cp = Compound).

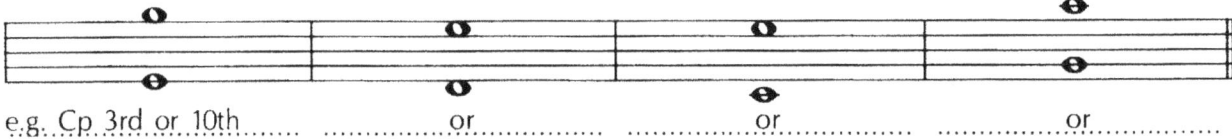

e.g. Cp 3rd or 10th .... or .... or .... or ....

(2) Write 9ths and 10ths above the given notes.

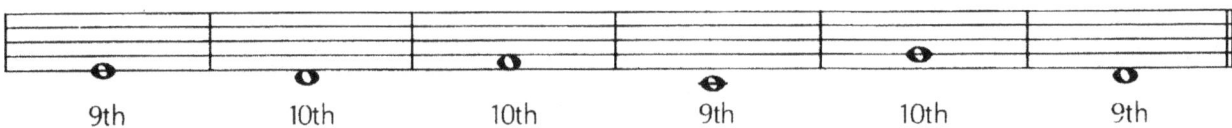

9th   10th   10th   9th   10th   9th

LESSON THREE

NOTE-NAMING EXERCISES USING COMPOUND INTERVALS AND LEGER LINE NOTES

Here is the alphabetical list of note names for you to use in the next questions. On it I have given examples of how to work out 9ths and 10ths.

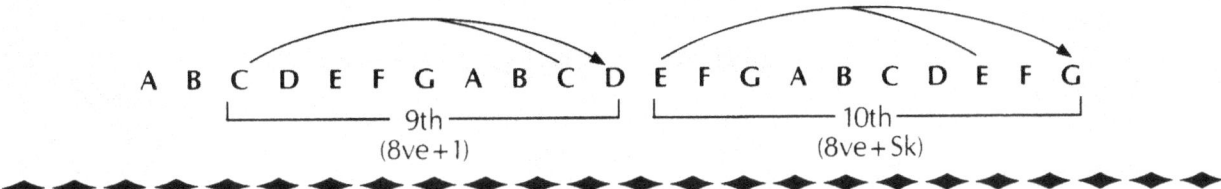

(1) First write the interval between each note in the space above the staff, as was done in Books 1 and 2. Next use the alphabetical list and the interval to work out the note names. Work from a Signpost C.

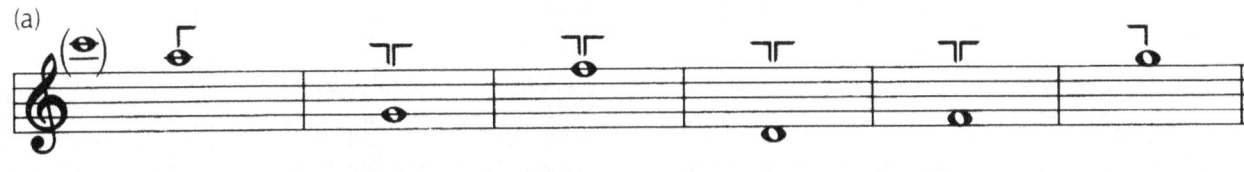

(2) Write the required notes on Leger Lines above or below the staff.

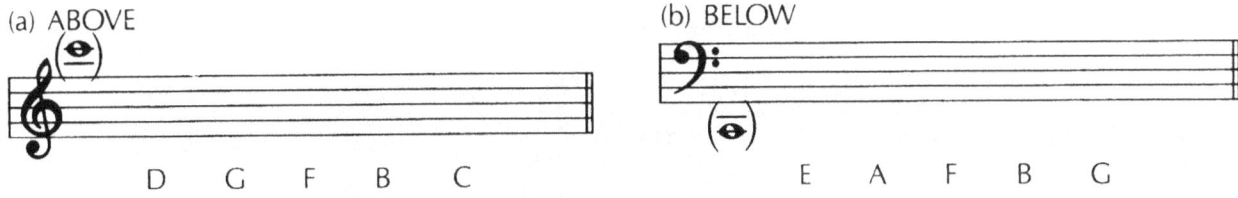

(3) Write the following notes by first working out the interval between each note name and writing it in between the brackets above the staff. The arrows show the direction in which the notes should move. Where Ninths and Tenths are required, the information has already been placed above the staff.

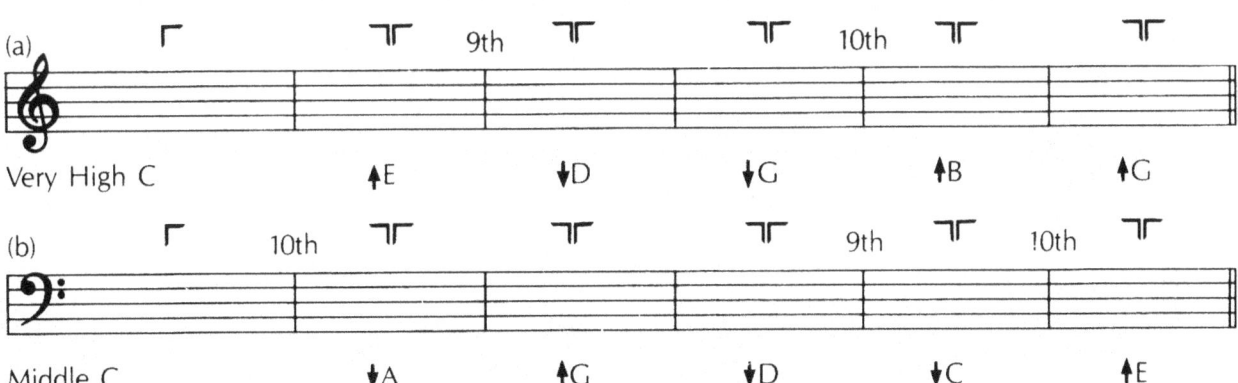

LESSON FOUR

THE DEMISEMIQUAVER OR 32ND NOTE

NOTE: ♪ MATCHING REST: ≋

The Demisemiquaver or 32nd note is the next smallest note value after the Semiquaver or 16th note. As you can see by the chart below, 32 of these notes take up the same time span as a Semibreve or Whole Note.

The **note** has **three tails** and the matching **rest** has **three hooks**.

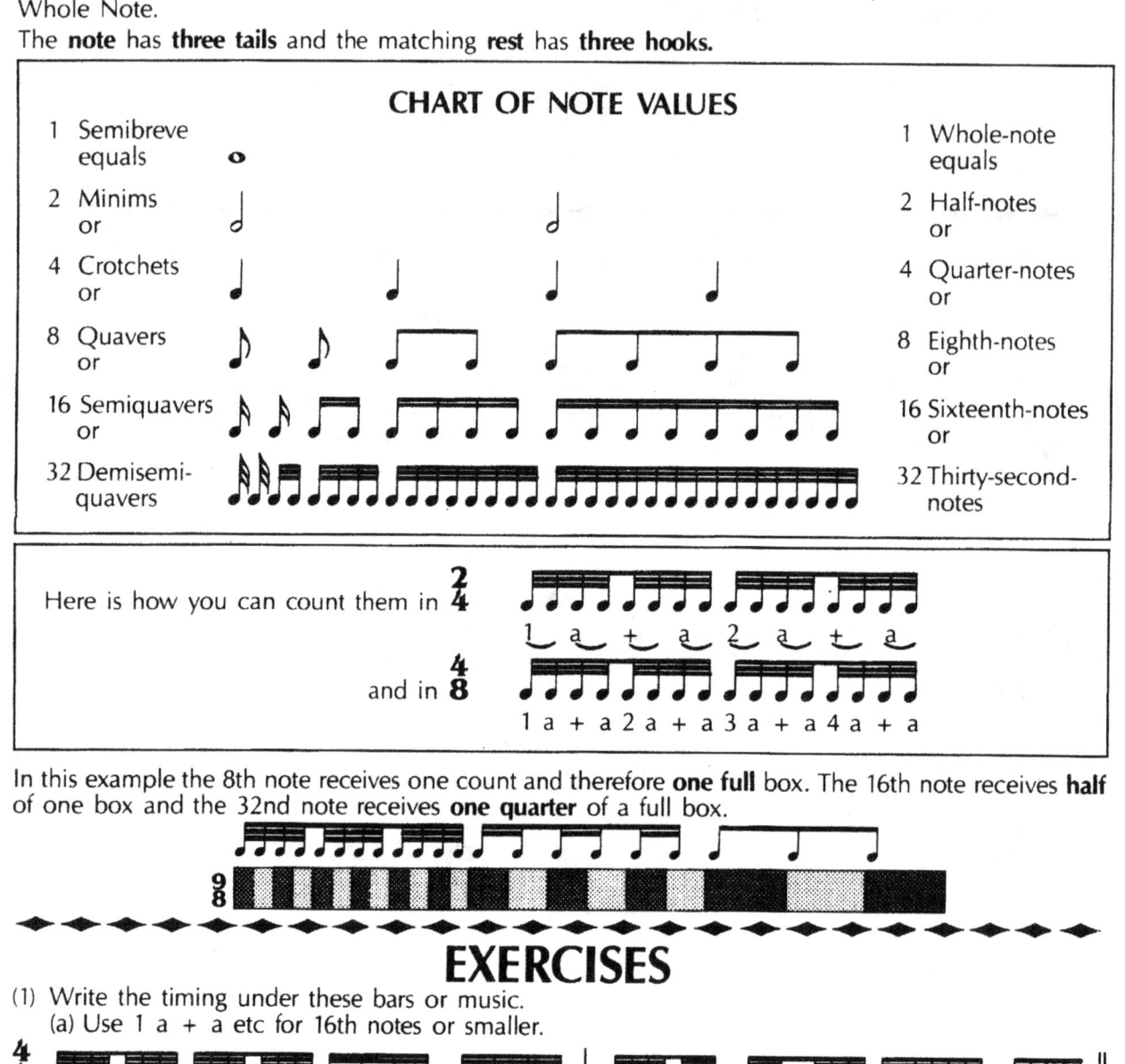

EXERCISES

(1) Write the timing under these bars or music.
 (a) Use 1 a + a etc for 16th notes or smaller.

 (b) Use 1 a + a etc for 32nd notes.

(2) First write the timing under the bars, then fill the bars with 32nd notes correctly grouped.

LESSON FIVE

RELATIVE MINOR SCALES
PART A — THE NATURAL MINOR SCALE

The Major and Minor Scales used in music today have their origins in the Medieval Church Modes or Scales. The basic forms of the Modes can be found by playing one octave of any white note group on a keyboard. That is, from D to D along the white notes or from F to F etc.

Over time, two white note scale sounds were favoured over the others. These were the sound of the scale from C to C (the Ionian Mode) which is now known as the Major Scale and the sound of the scale from A to A along the white notes (the Aeolian Mode) which is now known as the NATURAL MINOR SCALE. It is also known by other names such as the **Pure Minor scale** or the **Ancient Minor Scale**.

RELATIVE MINOR AND RELATIVE MAJOR SCALES

The relationship of the two white note scales C Major and A Natural Minor is that they both have no sharps or flats, in other words the same Key Signature, AND the Tonic Notes (starting notes of the scales) are the INTERVAL of a SIXTH apart.

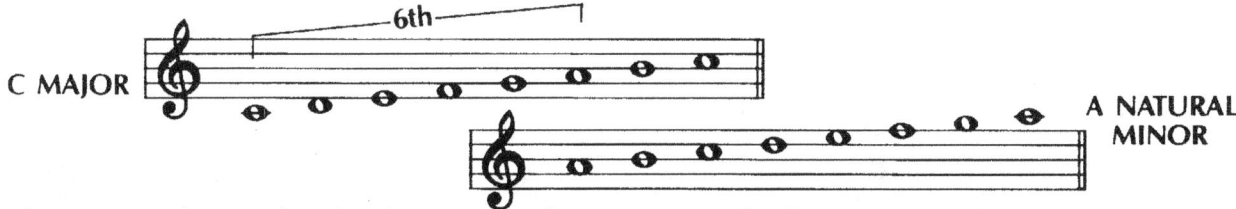

These two scales are therefore known as Relative Major and Relative Minor scales to each other.

The example above, provides us with a formula with which to work out all the other minor scales which have the same KEY SIGNATURE as their Relative Majors.

> REMEMBER THIS ONE SENTENCE. Then use it from which ever point of view applies.
> "THE RELATIVE MINOR IS FOUND ON THE **SIXTH** NOTE OF THE MAJOR SCALE"

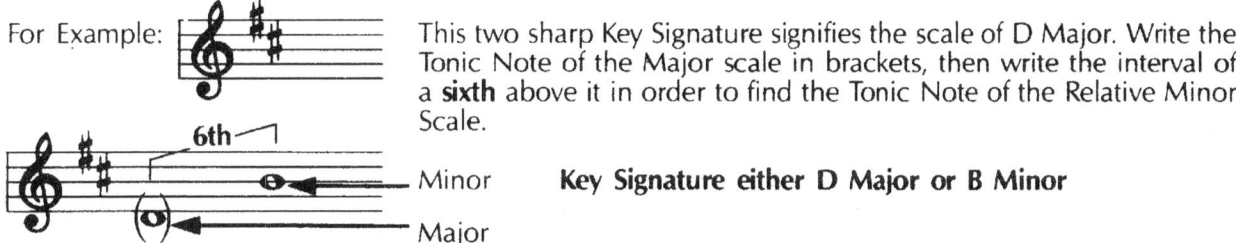

For Example: This two sharp Key Signature signifies the scale of D Major. Write the Tonic Note of the Major scale in brackets, then write the interval of a **sixth** above it in order to find the Tonic Note of the Relative Minor Scale.

Key Signature either D Major or B Minor

EXERCISE

Write one octave of the Natural Minor scales which have the following Key Signatures.
Follow the example given.

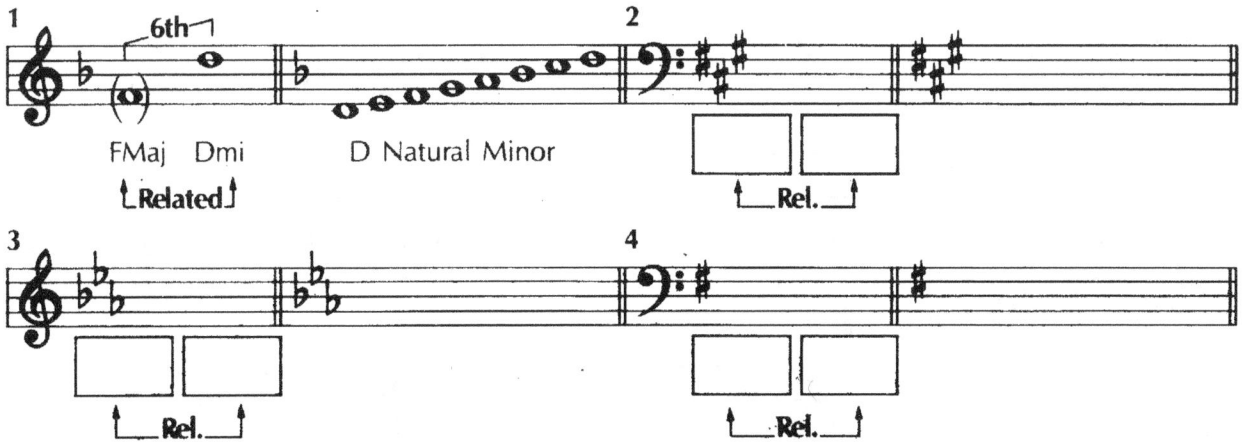

LESSON SIX

RELATIVE MINOR SCALES
PART B — THE HARMONIC MINOR SCALE

This form of the Minor Scale is the most frequently used form of the scale as it provides the basis for the chords or 'Harmony' used in Minor Keys. When many books refer to the Minor scale without stating the specific form, the Harmonic Minor is the scale that is being referred to.

The difference between the Natural Minor Scale and the Harmonic Minor Scale is that in the **Harmonic form** the SEVENTH note is **raised** by a **semitone**. When the 7th degree (note) is raised, the interval of a TONE AND A HALF (3 semitones) is created between the 6th and 7th degrees.

The Harmonic Minor scale is the only scale in common use that has this distinctive interval between two notes. All other Major and Minor scales use only Tones and Semitones.

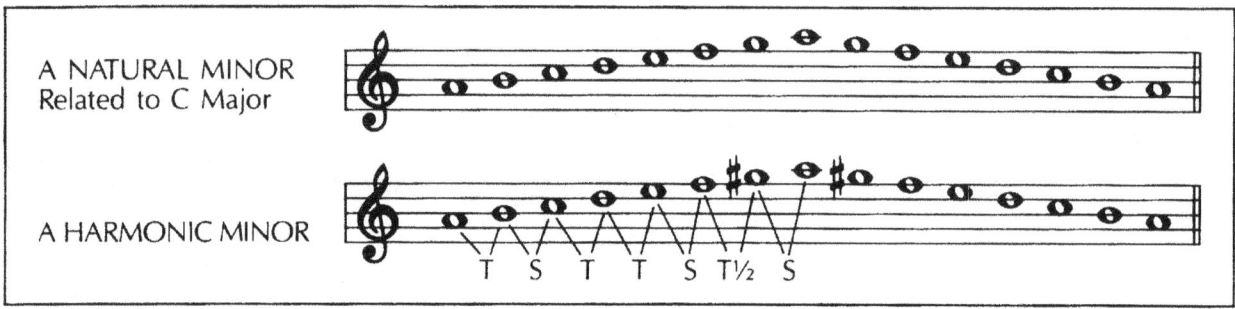

As you can see by the above example the formula for the Harmonic Minor Scale in tones and semitones is:

T S T T S T½ S

EXERCISES

(1) Write one octave ascending of each of these Relative Major and Relative Natural and Harmonic Minor Scales.

(2) Write one Octave of the Harmonic Minor Scales which have these Key Signatures. Do not forget to raise the 7th degree.

(♭ becomes ♮; ♮ becomes ♯)

LESSON SEVEN

MORE ON THE HARMONIC MINOR SCALE

As the Harmonic form of the minor scale is so frequently used, many people learn the scale formula for this scale in much the same way as they memorize the Major Scale formula.

Using the Harmonic Minor scale formula and the keyboard pathway for the scale, one can find the scale without reference to the Relative Major, if so desired.

The following questions require you to map out the Keyboard Pattern for the scale and then to alter the accidentals on the given ladder of notes as was done for the Major Scales in Book 1 of this series.

EXERCISES

(1) Find the keyboard pathway for F Harmonic Minor scale by placing a dot on each scale note and then joining the dots with curved lines. Follow the Harmonic Minor formula of: T S T T S T½ S

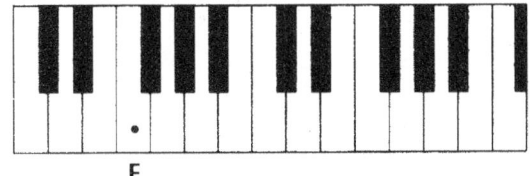 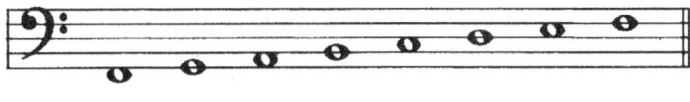

(2) Find the Keyboard pathway for G Harmonic Minor scale and add the necessary accidentals to the scale.

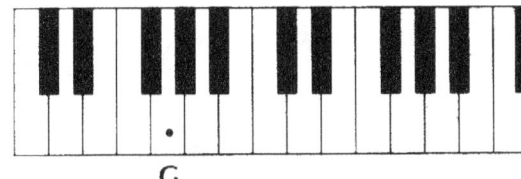 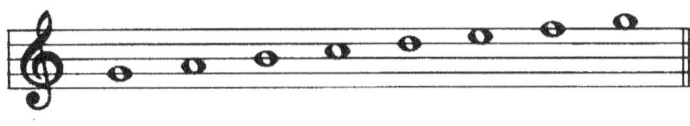

(3) Find the keyboard pathway for B Harmonic Minor scale and add the necessary accidentals to the scale.

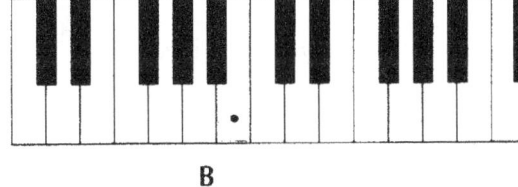 

(4) Following the Harmonic Minor scale formula write the scales beginning on the given notes without reference to the keyboard pathway.

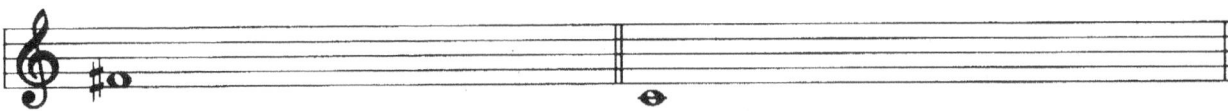

(5) Identify the following scales as Major, Natural Minor or Harmonic Minor Scales.

....

....

LESSON EIGHT

RELATIVE MINOR SCALES
PART C — THE MELODIC MINOR SCALE

The Harmonic Minor Scale discussed on the previous page, is rarely used when constructing a melody because the interval of a Tone and a Half (3 semitones) between the 6th and 7th degrees is an awkward interval to sing.

The **Melodic Minor** is another form of the minor scale. It is suitable for melodies as it avoids the awkward Tone and a Half interval.

In this form of the scale, both the 6th and the 7th degrees are raised in the ascending scale so that the intervals between the notes are only Tones or Semitones. In the descending form of the scale the notes are lowered so that the scale reverts to the Natural Minor form of the scale.

The Melodic Minor scale is easy to work out if you work it out from the Natural Minor form of the scale.

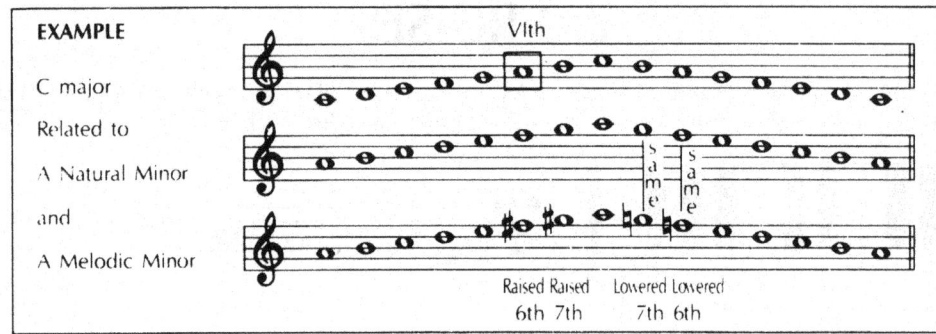

EXERCISES

(1) Add accidentals to alter these Natural Minor scales so that they become Melodic Minor scales.

(2) Write the Natural and Melodic forms of the minor scales with the following Key Signatures.

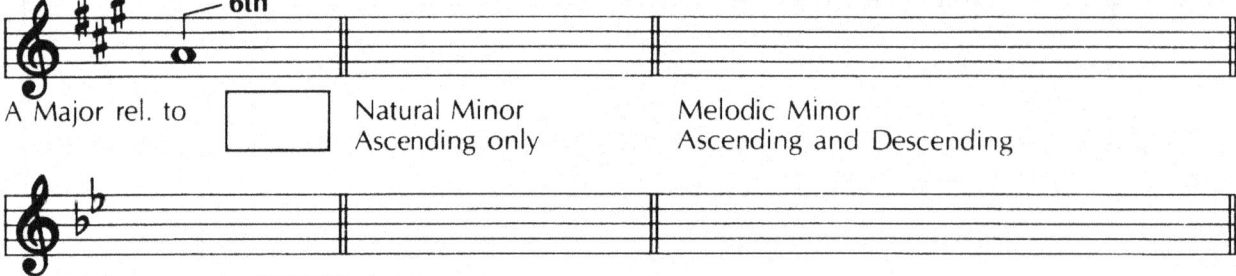

(3) Write the accidentals on these scales to form the type of scale required.

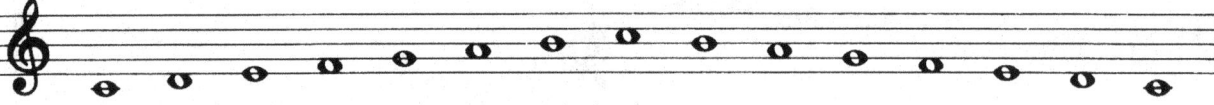

Melodic form

LESSON NINE

THE FULL CYCLE OF FIFTHS INCLUDING MINOR KEYS

Here is the Cycle of Fifths showing the Relative Minor Keys in the middle circle. The keys to the right move **up** by Fifths while the keys to the left move **down** by Fifths.

The numbers on the inner circle indicate the number of Sharps or Flats in each Key signature.

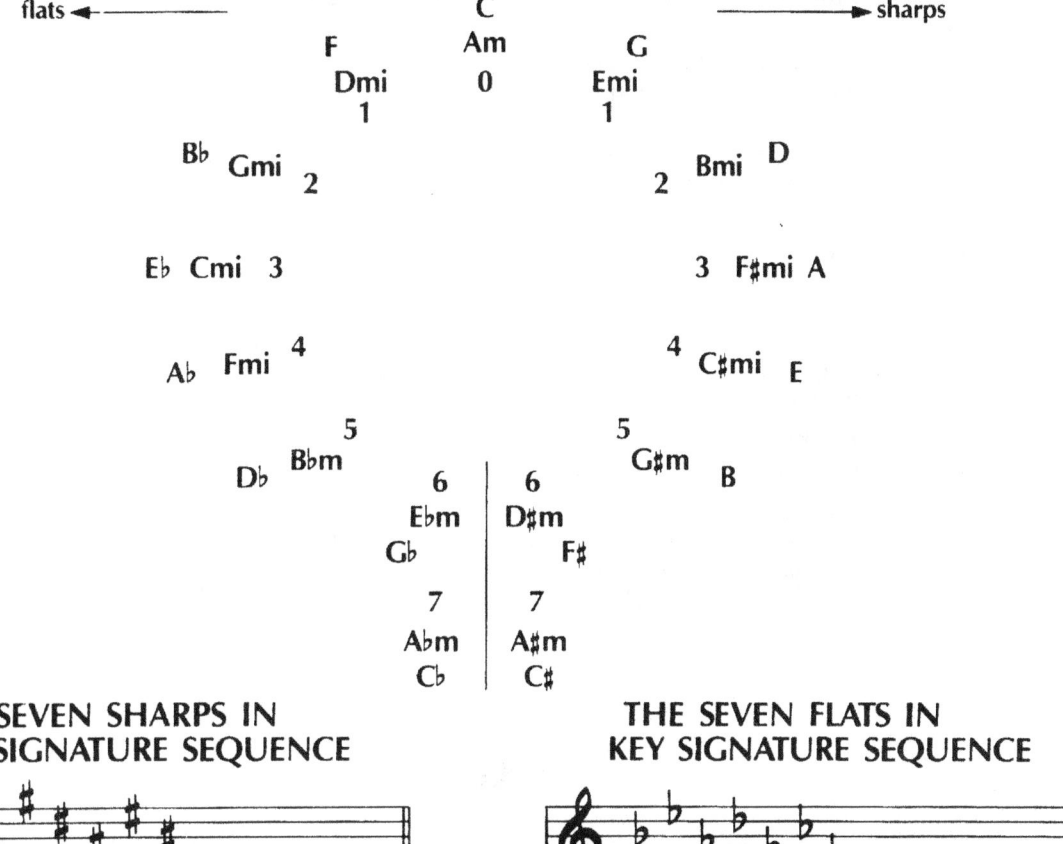

THE SEVEN SHARPS IN KEY SIGNATURE SEQUENCE

THE SEVEN FLATS IN KEY SIGNATURE SEQUENCE

RELATIVE MAJOR KEYS

If you know the Tonic Note of the Minor Scale and wish to work out the Relative Major Key, you can still use the method learned in Lesson Six. THE RELATIVE MINOR IS FOUND ON THE SIXTH NOTE OF THE MAJOR SCALE.

Therefore to find the Relative Major easily, go up a TONE to the 7th degree of the scale and then another SEMITONE to the Upper Tonic of the Major Scale. For Example:

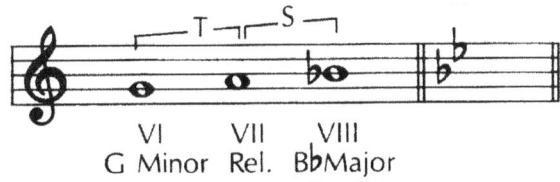

G Minor Rel. B♭ Major

EXERCISE

Find the Relative Major Keys to these Tonic Notes of Minor Scales, then write the Key Signatures.

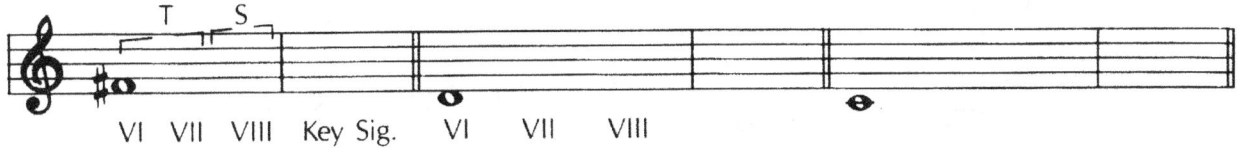

LESSON TEN

HOW TO ASSESS THE KEY OF A MELODY

Section One — When the Key Signature is present
There are three steps to take:

1 — Look at the number of sharps or flats in the Key Signature.

2 — In a single line melody the last note of the tune will be the Tonic note of the scale in the majority of cases.

   — In a harmonised melody where chords are present below the melody line, the lowest note of the final Root Position chord will be the Root Note of the chord and the Tonic Note of the scale.

3 — If you think the melody is in the Minor key, check for accidentals indicating the Raised Seventh degree (Harmonic Minor) or the Raised Sixth and Raised Seventh degrees (Melodic Minor).

Section Two — When the Key Signature is absent
There are four steps to take:

1 — Gather together the accidentals to form a Key Signature. Remember that if there are several notes with the same name which have the same accidental placed in front of them, that the accidental is counted only **once** in the Key Signature.

   — Any accidentals which do not fit into the key signature pattern are likely to be the Raised Notes found in the Minor forms of the scale.

   — If the melody touches upon most of the accidentals, but happens to leave out one, use your Key Signature knowledge to supply the missing accidental. e.g. If you see B♭, E♭ and D♭ you would realise that the Key Signature would need to be A♭ Major (4 flats) because the Key Signature sequence always uses A♭ before D♭ (B♭, E♭, A♭, D♭).

Steps 2, 3 and 4 are the same as steps 1, 2 and 3 in Section One.

◆◆◆◆◆◆◆◆◆◆◆◆◆◆◆◆◆◆◆◆◆◆◆◆◆◆◆◆◆◆

EXERCISES

(1) Assess the key of this melody. Key = ...

(2) Assess the key of this melody. Key = ...

(3) First gather together the accidentals to form a Key Signature then indicate the key of this melody.

   Key = ...

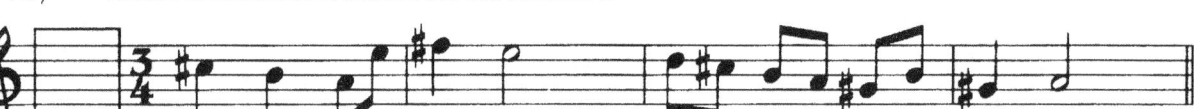

(4) Write the Key Signature for this melody and then indicate the key. Key = ...

LESSON ELEVEN
TONIC MINOR SCALES

Sometimes in a piece of music the sound will change abruptly from the Major Scale sound on the Keynote, to the Minor Scale sound on the same Keynote. When this happens the music is said to move from the Tonic Major scale to the Tonic Minor scale. For example from C Major scale (0♯'s, 0♭'s) to C Minor Scale (3♭'s), **not** to the Relative Minor Scale (A Minor).

> **The difference in the Key Signature between a Tonic Major and Tonic Minor Scale is that from the Major to the Minor there are either THREE SHARPS LESS or THREE FLATS MORE.**

e.g.   F♯ Major — 6 sharps;   F♯ Minor — 3 sharps   (6 – 3 = 3 Sharps)
       B Major — 5 sharps;   B Minor — 2 sharps   (5 – 3 = 2 Sharps)
       F Major — 1 Flat;   F Minor — 4 Flats   (1 + 3 = 4 Flats)
       E♭ Major — 3 Flats;   E♭ Minor — 6 Flats;   (3 + 3 = 6 Flats)

Another way to view this connection, is to see the Key Signature of the Tonic Minor as being the same as the Major Key Signature THREE Moves to the LEFT around the Cycle of Fifths.

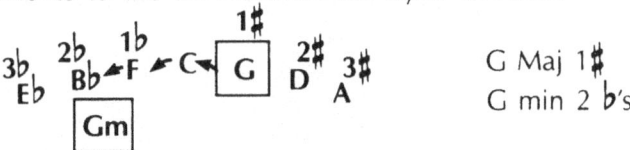

G Maj 1♯
G min 2♭'s

C Minor has the same Key Signature as E♭ Major (3 Flats)
G Minor has the same Key Signature as B♭ Major (2 Flats)

A Third way in which to find the Key Signature of the Tonic Minor Scale, is to lower the 3rd, 6th and 7th degrees of the Major Scale by a SEMITONE each. This will produce the Natural Minor form of the scale.

◆ ◆

EXERCISES

(1) Write the Tonic Major and Tonic Natural and Harmonic Minor scales beginning on the given note. Use Accidentals

(2) Write the Key Signatures of the following Major and Minor keys.

LESSON TWELVE

MORE REPEAT SIGNS AND ASSOCIATED TERMS

In addition to the Repeat Sign ||: :|| and 1st and 2nd endings ||: |1. :||2. | covered in Book One of this series, there are several other signs which indicate that a player should repeat a section or skip over to another section.

TERM	MEANING
Da Capo (D.C.)	— return to the head or beginning of the piece
Dal Segno (D.S.) 𝄋	— return to the sign
Fine (pronounced Fee-nay)	— the end
Coda	— literally 'tailpiece'; a short passage which concludes a work, often indicated by the Coda sign
Coda sign ⊕	
Poi Coda	— then Coda

Full instructions you may see are:

Da Capo al Fine: This means return to the beginning then finish where you see the word Fine, or simply the end of the piece if the word Fine is not present.

Dal Segno al Coda ⊕ poi Coda: This means return to the sign (𝄋) then play as far as the coda sign (⊕) in the body piece, then go straight to the Coda section at the end of the piece, which is again marked with a matching Coda sign.

OTHER SIGNS	MEANING
./.	— repeat the previous bar
.//.	— repeat the previous two bars
(4 bar rest)	— multiple bar rest, used to indicate two or more bars rest, depending on the number placed above it.
♩ with slash	— shorthand for four quavers in instrumental music ♩ = ♫♫
♩ with double slash	— shorthand for four semiquavers ♩ = ♬♬
♩ with triple slash	— usually indicates a tremolo which for string players is a very rapid bowing effect
M.M. ♩ = 60	— M.M. = Maelzel's Metronome. Number = speed setting. Note-value = type of note which receives **one** beat. N.B. 60 = 1 beat/second; 120 = two beats/second.

◆◆◆◆◆◆◆◆◆◆◆◆◆◆◆◆◆◆◆◆◆◆◆◆

EXERCISES

Complete these sentences.

(1) **Fine** means ....

(2) **Dal segno** means ....

(3) The Italian term which means return to the beginning is ....

(4) ./. means ....

(5) The short passage at the end of a work is called a ....

(6) | **8** | means ....

LESSON THIRTEEN

TRANSPOSITION

To transpose a piece of music means to place it in its entirety into a new key. A piece in a Major Key can only transpose to another Major Key, while a piece in a Minor Key can likewise only be transposed to another Minor Key.

THE ART OF TRANSPOSITION is simple if you approach it from the intervallic point of view. There are **three** steps to be followed:

(1) Find the key of the original piece, using the Key Signature and the **final note** as a guide.
    In a single line melody the final note is almost always the Tonic of the Key. In a harmonised piece (2 parts or more) the **Tonic** will be the Root Note of the final chord, which is always a Root Position chord. Therefore the Tonic will be the **lowest** sounding note of that chord.

(2) Find the starting degree of the piece (3rd or 5th degree of the scale etc). Then find the same degree of the Key in which you wish to transpose the piece.

(3) Match the intervals between each note as you move along the line, making sure that you finish on the same degree as the original tune. (Most probably it will be the Tonic.)

EXAMPLE
Original Tune in D Major

Transpose up a 5th to A Major

EXERCISES

(1) Indicate the key, starting degree and finishing degree of the following piece. Key ....

    Starting Degree .... Finishing degree ....

(2) Write the intervals between each note in the brackets above.

(3) Transpose this piece down a 4th to the key of F Major. First write the Key Signature, Time Signature and starting degree at the beginning of the staff lines. Then move by intervals from each note to the next. Where there are added accidentals in the original tune, simply add them in the same place in the transposed piece. Make sure that the stems are correct for the new positions of the notes and that the rhythmic values match the original melody.

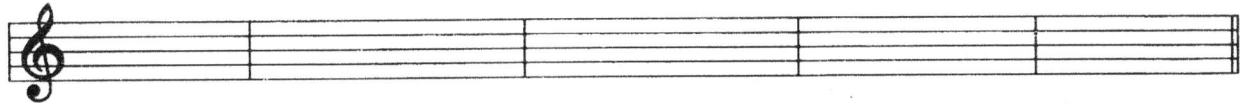

LESSON FOURTEEN

MINOR SCALE AND TRANSPOSITION REVIEW

(1) Name the Relative Minor Keys to the given notes.

e.g. E C♯m

(2) Name the Relative Major Keys to these Tonic Notes of Minor Keys. Then write in the Key Signatures.

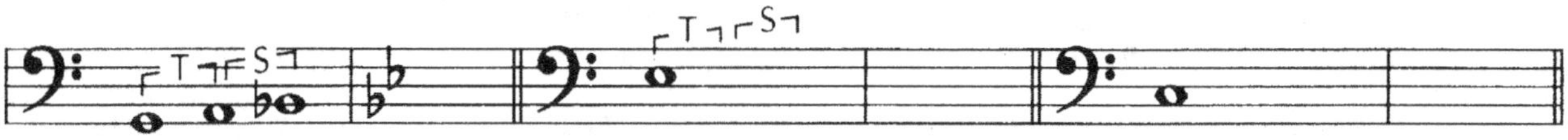

Gm = B♭ = 2 Flats   Em = ... = ...

(3) Identify the following scales as either Major or Natural Minor. Don't forget to supply the letter-name for each scale.

(4) Identify the following scales as either Natural, Harmonic or Melodic Minor scales.

(a)

(b)

(5) Write the Tonic Major and Tonic Minor scales beginning on the following notes. Use Accidentals.

Tonic Major   Tonic Minor (Harmonic Form)

(6) Write the three forms of the minor scale beginning on D. Use Accidentals.

Natural   Harmonic

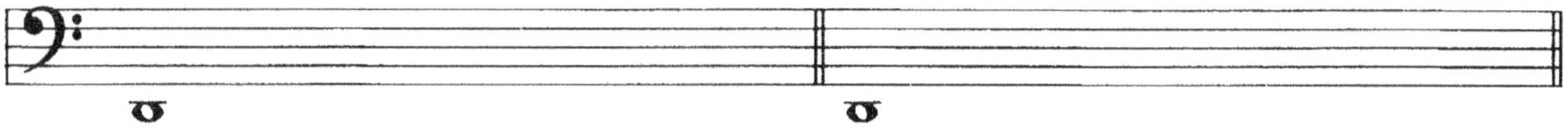

Melodic

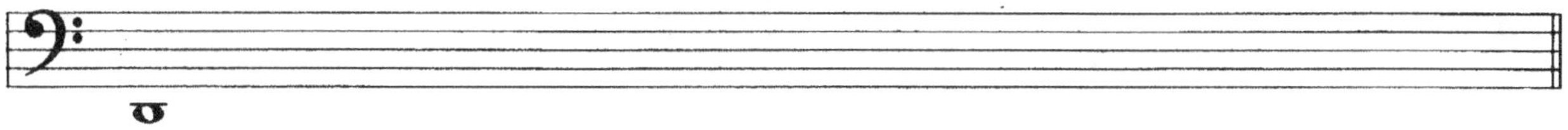

(7) Transpose this minor melody, to the key of C minor, a third higher.

Key: ...... Starting Degree ☐   Finishing Degree ☐

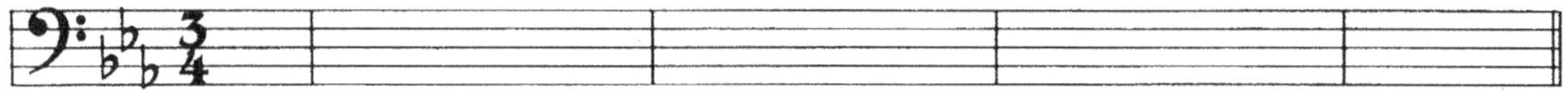

LESSON FIFTEEN

SIMPLE METER TIME SIGNATURES (REVIEW)

SIMPLE TIME

SIMPLE DUPLE — Two **undotted** Beat Notes per bar

SIMPLE TRIPLE — Three **undotted** Beat Notes per bar

Count: 1 + 2 + 3 +

SIMPLE QUADRUPLE — Four **undotted** Beat Notes per bar

Count: 1 + 2 + 3 + 4 +

Colour highlight the lower number of each time signature for lessons 15 - 20, using the standard colours.

> A Simple Time Signature can be defined as a Time-Signature in which THE BEAT NOTE IS UNDOTTED, dividing into TWO equal parts or pulses.

The Time Signatures which use the 1/2, 1/4 and 1/8th notes as Beat Notes, were discussed in Book One of this series. Further possibilities using the 1/16th, 1/32nd and 1/64th notes are presented on the right hand section of the chart.

All these Time Signatures are written in terms of Beat Notes; that is, each Beat Note receives one number while the pulses are counted as 'ANDS'

◆◆◆◆◆◆◆◆◆◆◆◆◆◆◆◆◆◆◆◆◆◆◆◆◆

EXERCISES

Draw in the bar lines and write in the timing for these lines of music.

(1)

(2)

(3)

19

LESSON SIXTEEN

COMPOUND METER TIME SIGNATURES
COMPOUND TIME

A Compound Time Signature can be defined as any Time-Signature in which THE BEAT NOTE IS DOTTED, dividing into THREE equal parts or pulses.

Examples of the types of Beat Notes are Dotted Minims (Half Notes) 𝅗𝅥., Dotted Crotchets (Quarter Notes) ♩., and Dotted Quavers (Eighth Notes) ♪.

In any Compound Time Signature the Time Signature is written in terms of the **pulse**. That is, each pulse receives one number, rather than each Beat Note.
The above chart demonstrates how this works.

GROUPING — When grouping notes and rests in Compound Time Signatures make sure that they agree with the Dotted Beat Notes and fall into groups of **three**.
The exception is when one note or rest occupies are full bar. e.g. 6/8 𝅗𝅥.
Any Time Signatures in the Compound Duple and Compound Quadruple categories should be grouped in two halves, with an imaginary bar line down the middle.

Do not cross the middle of the bar when combining note values.

20

LESSON SEVENTEEN

MORE ON COMPOUND METER TIME SIGNATURES

Grouping of Rests

As in previous Time Signatures with three beats per bar, a combined rest should be used for the first and second units, while separate rests should be used for the second and third units.
In Compound Time Signatures always group rests to agree with the Dotted Beat Notes and keep the above information in mind.
Also remember that the Semibreve Rest or Whole Rest should be used for a WHOLE BAR'S REST in any Time Signature.

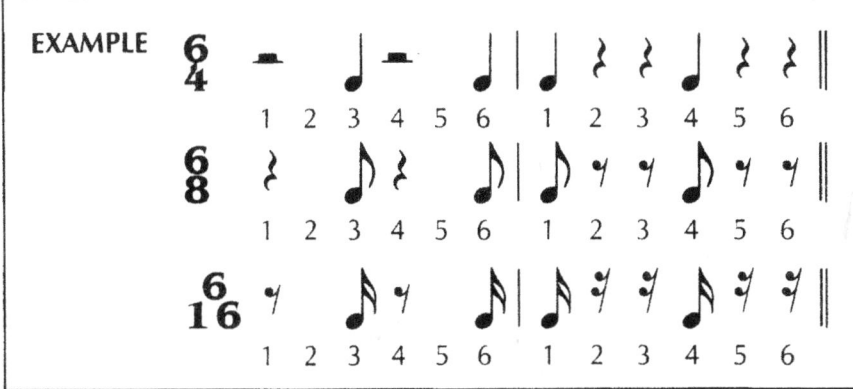

Combined Rest on counts 1 and 2 or 4 and 5.

Separate Rests on counts 2 and 3 or 5 and 6.

Dotted Rests may be used in the same situations as Dotted Notes.

EXERCISES

(1) Write the counts under these bars of rhythm.

(2) First write the counts under the bars then fill the bars with notes and rests.

(3) Divide these lines into bars and write in the timing.

LESSON EIGHTEEN
THE TRIPLET

A **Triplet** is a group of **three** notes played in the time of one note of the next larger value.

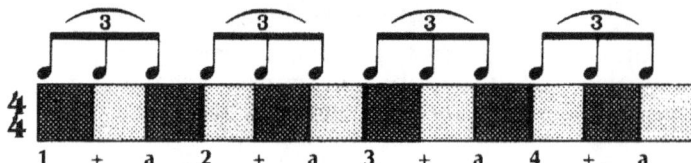

Triplets are used in Simple Time Signatures where the **usual** subdivision of each Beat Note is into **two** pulses.

The sign used to indicate a TRIPLET is a curved or square bracket with the number 3 inside it. Do not confuse the curved bracket with the curved slur line.

Quaver and Semiquaver Triplets usually use the curved bracket while Crotchet Triplets use the square bracket.

To count triplets say the number plus the unit '+ a' *(and uh)*.

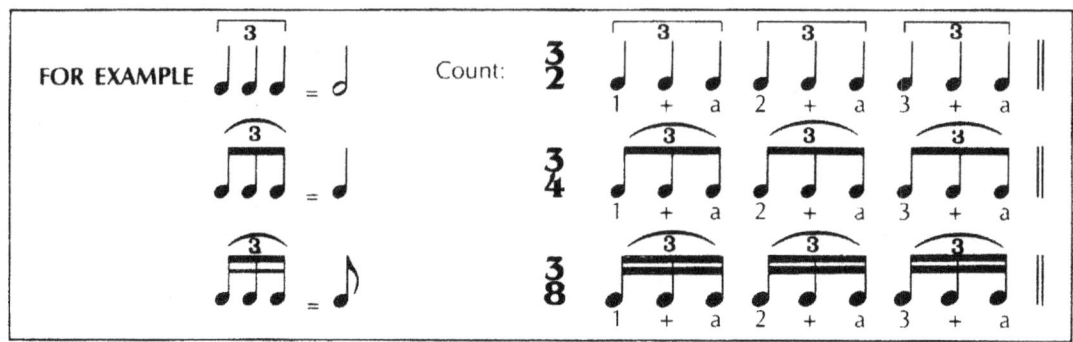

EVEN TRIPLETS — In the majority of cases the Triplet consists of three notes of the same value, and is known as an **Even** Triplet.

UNEVEN TRIPLETS — Sometimes the combined value of the three triplet notes is altered so that within the triplet bracket there may be longer or shorter note values. These are some examples of Uneven Triplets:

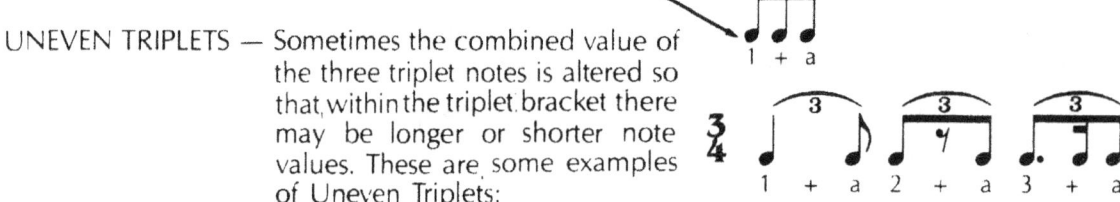

MUSIC THAT SOUNDS AS IF EACH BEAT NOTE CAN BE DIVIDED INTO THREE PARTS CAN BE WRITTEN IN TWO WAYS.

1. Using a Compound Time Signature.   2. Using a Simple Time Signature and employing the Triplet sign.

Note that uneven groups of **three** from the Compound Time Signature can be written out exactly the same way using the Triplet·Sign in the Simple Time Signature.

EXAMPLE These lines of music will sound the same.

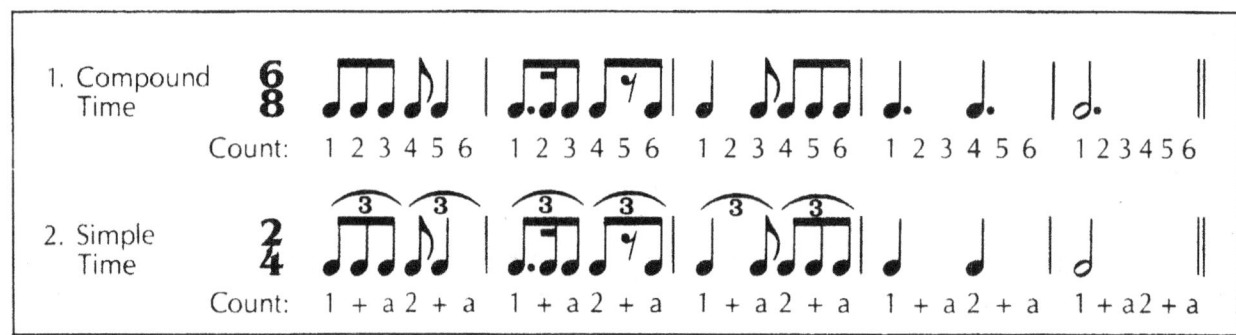

LESSON NINETEEN
THE DUPLET

A **Duplet** is a group of **two** notes played in the time of one dotted note of the next larger value.

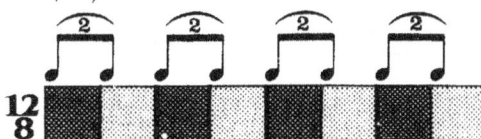

Duplets are used in Compound Time Signatures where the **usual** subdivision of each Beat Note is into **three** pulses.
The sign used to indicate a Duplet is either the curved or square bracket over the number 2.

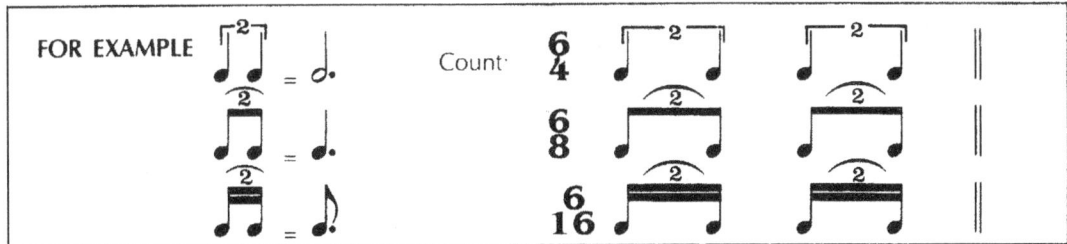

The Duplet can be counted in two ways:

(a) For example in 6/8 by changing the counting in the bar from

1 2 3 4 5 6 over to 1 + 2 +

or (b) by counting 1 + 2 + 3 + 4 + 5 + 6 + and sounding the Duplet Notes where shown in this bar.

MUSIC THAT SOUNDS AS IF EACH BEAT CAN BE DIVIDED INTO TWO PARTS CAN ALSO BE WRITTEN IN TWO WAYS.

1. Using a Simple Meter Time Signature.
2. Using a Compound Meter Time Signature and employing the Duplet sign.

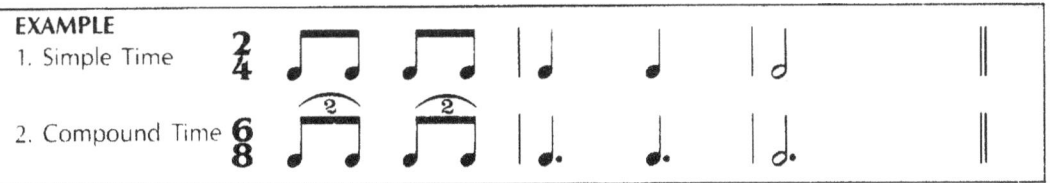

EXERCISES

(1) Rewrite this music in 3/4 using the Triplet Sign as needed.   9/8 𝅗𝅥. = 3/4 𝅗𝅥

(2) Rewrite this music in 6/8 using the Duplet Sign as needed.   6/8 𝅗𝅥. = 2/4 𝅗𝅥

LESSON TWENTY

REVIEW OF TIME SIGNATURES
TRIPLETS AND DUPLETS

EXERCISES

(1) Referring to the chart of Time Signatures in Lessons 15 and 16, give the equivalent Compound Time Signatures to these Simple Time Signatures. e.g. The equivalent Compound Time Signature to 3/4, which uses 3 **Undotted** Crotchet Beat Notes is 9/8 which uses 3 **Dotted** Crotchet Beat Notes.

(a) 2/4 = ☐   (b) 3/2 = ☐   (c) 4/8 = ☐   (d) 2/2 = ☐

(2) Give the equivalent Simple Time Signatures to these Compound Time Signatures.

(a) 9/8 = ☐   (b) 6/16 = ☐   (c) 12/4 = ☐   (d) 12/8 = ☐

(3) Rewrite this music grouping the quavers to agree with the Time Signatures. Refer to the chart if you need to. Write the Timing under the bars first.

6/8 | | | | ||

3/4 | | | . | ||

(4) Write the Timing under these bars in Simple Time which use most note values including the Quaver Triplet.

(5) Write the Timing under these bars in Compound Time which also include the Quaver Duplet.

6/8 ...

1 + 2 + 3 + 4 + 5 + 6 +

LESSON TWENTY-ONE

MODULATION

To **modulate** means to **change key**.

Most straightforward classical music and a great deal of popular music follows a general formula for changing key. If pieces do not follow this procedure they will of course have a more unusual sound.

The usual procedure when modulating is to move to a Key Signature that is either one sharp or flat **greater** or one sharp or flat **less** than the original key.

Using your knowledge of the movement of keys by FIFTHS, as in the Cycle of Fifths, you can plot the keys in this manner:

ORIGINAL KEY
D MAJOR (2♯'s)

MODULATION POINTS

	One Sharp less	Orig. Key	One Sharp more
	1♯	2♯'s	3♯'s
Major	G ———————	D ———————	A
Rel. Minor	Em	Bm	F♯m

ORIGINAL KEY
G MINOR (2♭'s)

MODULATION POINTS

	One Flat more	Orig. Key	One Flat less
	3♭'s	2♭'s	1♭
Minor	Cm ———————	Gm ———————	Dm
Rel. Major	E♭	B♭	F

If your original key is a Major Key, write the Major Keys on the top row and the Relative Minors underneath. If your original key is a Minor Key, write the Minors on the top row and the Relative Majors underneath. The lines forming the shape of the Letter 'T' indicate the most likely keys that the piece would travel to. The other keys are regarded as slightly more distant modulations.

◆◆◆◆◆◆◆◆◆◆◆◆◆◆◆◆◆◆◆◆◆◆

EXERCISES

(1) Complete the Modulation Points for these keys:
   Refer to the full Cycle of Fifths in Lesson Nine if you need to refresh your memory of Key Signatures.

2♯s	3♯'s	4♯'s
......	A	......
......	......	......

2♭s	1♭	0♭'s
......	Dm	......
......	......	......

0♯s	1♯	2♯'s
......	G	......
......	......	......

(2) Complete the number of sharps or flats and then the remainder of the spaces to indicate the Modulation Points for the given keys.

Number of Sharps or Flats:

......	......	......
......	C	......
......	......	......

......	......	......
......	Fm	......
......	......	......

Refer to the CTW2 page on www.margaretbrandman.com for the colour coding for each of the six keys that appear in the modulation point box.

LESSON TWENTY-TWO
MORE ON MODULATION

Here is an example of how to assess the Modulations in a short tune.

(1) Write the Modulation Points for the key.

KEY D MAJOR

	1♯	2♯'s	3♯'s
Majors	G	D	A
Minors	Em	Bm	F♯m

(2) Add the Accidentals to the Key Signature for each bracketted segment.

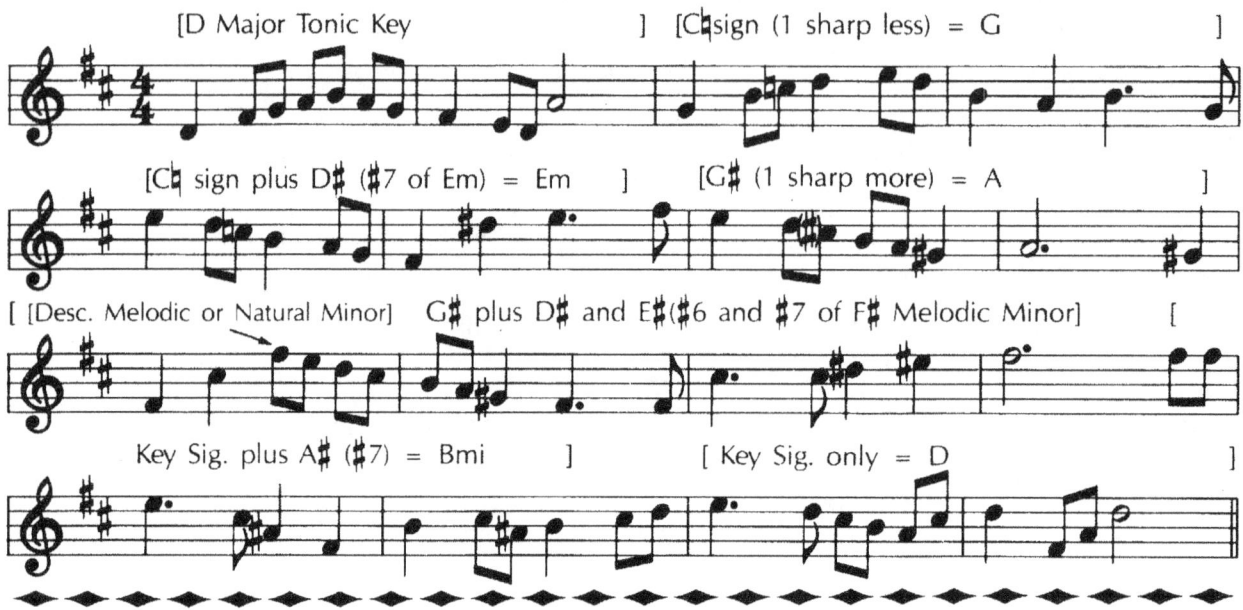

EXERCISE

(a) First write the Modulation Points or this tune.
(b) Then mark in the modulations between the brackets above the music. Add or subtract the accidentals in the music to the key signature for each segment. Don't forget that Minor Keys will have both the Key Signature accidentals plus either the Raised 7th (Harmonic Minor) or the Raised 6th and 7th (Melodic Minor) degrees.

Modulation Points:

LESSON TWENTY-THREE

INTERVAL QUALITIES

PERFECT AND MAJOR

Thus far in this series we have looked at intervals purely from the point of view of the visual distance between the notes.

A 3rd, 5th and 7th you will recall are written from Line Note to Line Note or Space Note to Space Note. The 2nd, 4th, 6th and 8ve are written from Line Note to Space Note or vice-versa.

SOUND

Each of these intervals takes on a different sound depending upon whether it occurs between the Tonic Note and another note of the Major Scale or not.

When building intervals we can use the MAJOR SCALE as a point of reference. Intervals which occur between the Tonic Note of a Major Scale and any other note above it in the scale, are known as either PERFECT or MAJOR Intervals.

PERFECT INTERVALS

Four of the Intervals found from the Tonic Note of the Major Scale are known as **Perfect Intervals**.

They are: the Perfect Prime or Unison (P1), the Perfect Fourth (P4)
the Perfect Fifth (P5) and the Perfect Octave (P8).

They have a smooth sound and when inverted (turned upside down) remain Perfect intervals.

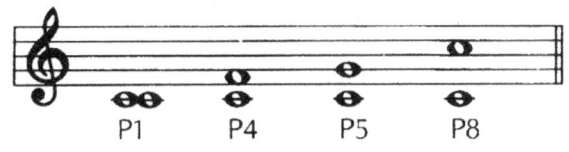

MAJOR INTERVALS

The other four intervals found from the Tonic Note of the Major Scale are known as **Major Intervals**. When referring to intervals the word Major literally means the '**greater** or larger' interval.

The four Major Intervals are: the Major Second (M2) the Major Third (M3)
the Major Sixth (M6) and the Major Seventh (M7).

EXERCISE

(1) Name these intervals built on the Tonic Note of G Scale.

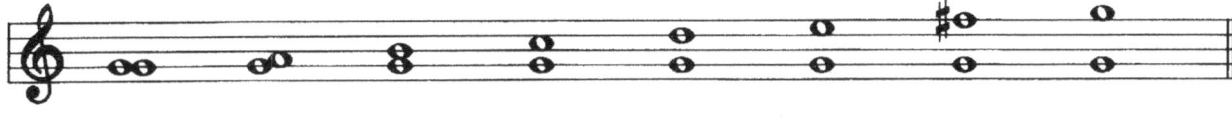

(2) Build these intervals above D. When writing these, regard D as the Tonic Note of the scale and keep in mind that the sharps of the Key Signature will need to be written in on the appropriate notes.

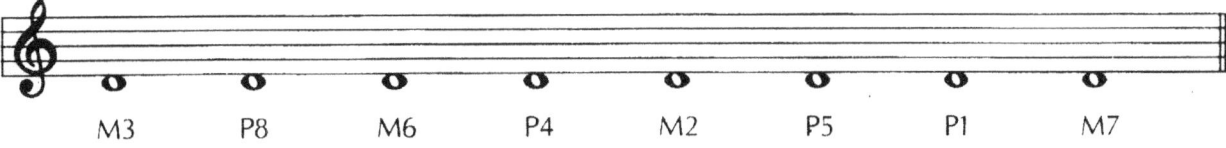

LESSON TWENTY-FOUR

INTERVAL QUALITIES

MINOR INTERVALS

The word '**Minor**' when applied to intervals literally means '**lesser**' as opposed to the Major or 'greater' intervals seen on the previous page. **Minor Intervals do not necessarily occur in Minor scales.**

The method of finding a **minor** interval is an easy one. Take any Major Interval and simply lower the upper note by a semitone.

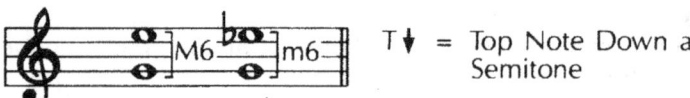

T↓ = Top Note Down a Semitone

Alternatively, if the lower note is not given as the keynote of the scale, you can raise the lower note by a semitone to bring the notes closer together.

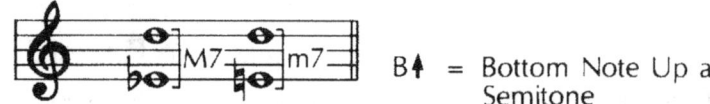

B↑ = Bottom Note Up a Semitone

Here are both the Major (M) and minor (m) Intervals written above C.

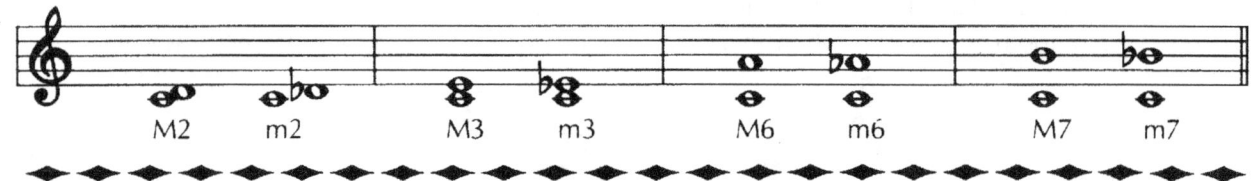

EXERCISES

(1) Change these intervals from Major to Minor by lowering the **top** note by a semitone. T↓

(2) Change these intervals from Major to Minor by raising the lower note by a semitone. B↑

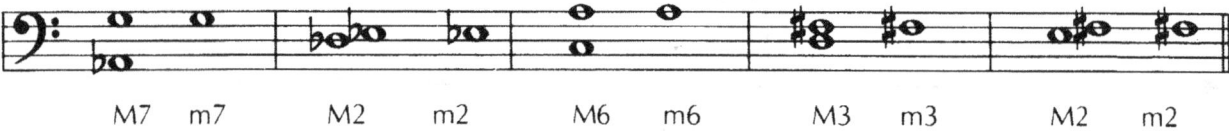

(3) Write Minor Intervals above the given notes.
Keep in mind that the lower note of each interval (the given note) indicates the scale from which you should work. Find the Major interval first then lower the upper note by a semitone.

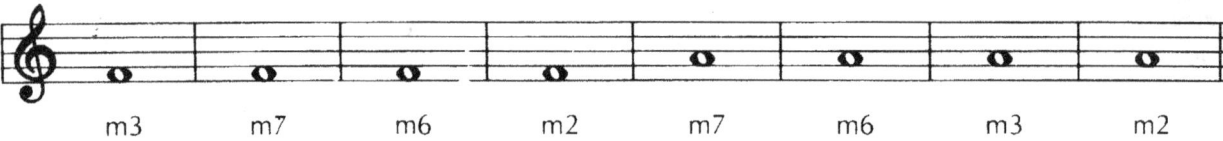

(4) Indicate both the size and the quality of these intervals. (Quality = Perfect, Major or Minor)

LESSON TWENTY-FIVE

INTERVAL QUALITIES

DIMINISHED INTERVALS

Any of the intervals thus far mentioned can be **made smaller** or '**diminished**' by following this formula:

PERFECT to DIMINISHED — Bring the interval closer by **one** semitone.
MINOR to DIMINISHED — Bring the interval closer by **one** semitone.
MAJOR to DIMINISHED — Bring the interval closer by **two** semitones.

In the following chart an arrow represents one semitone. T = Top. B = Bottom.

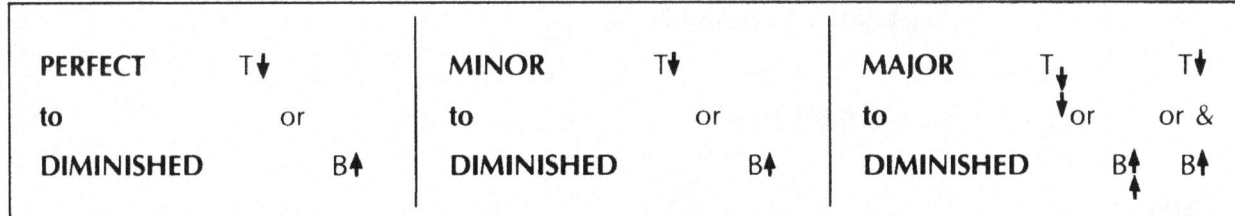

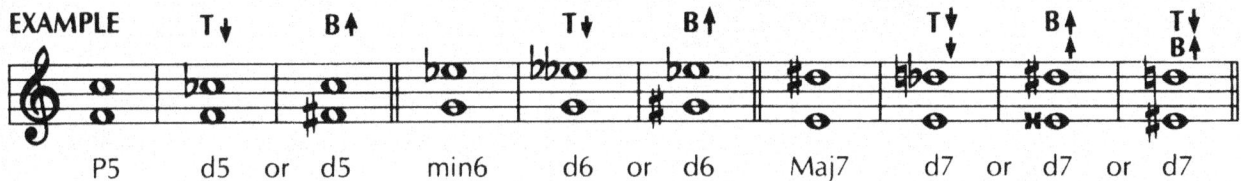

As you can see by the example above, when writing Diminished intervals sharps and flats may be used in the same interval.

◆◆◆◆◆◆◆◆◆◆◆◆◆◆◆◆◆◆◆◆◆◆◆◆◆◆◆◆

EXERCISES

(1) Change these intervals from Perfect to Diminished or from Minor to Diminished. Take either the Top Note down a semitone (T↓) or the Bottom Note up a semitone (B↑) depending upon which note is fixed. Write the names of all the intervals in the spaces below.

(2) Change these intervals from Major to Diminished. T↓ or B↑ OR T↓ and B↑.
Name all intervals in the spaces below.

(3) Write the following intervals ABOVE the given notes.

LESSON TWENTY-SIX

INTERVAL QUALITIES

AUGMENTED INTERVALS

The Perfect and Major intervals can be converted to larger intervals or '**augmented**' intervals by following this formula:

PERFECT to AUGMENTED — Make the interval larger by **one** semitone.
MAJOR to AUGMENTED — Make the interval larger by **one** semitone.

THAT IS: follow the same procedure for both types of interval.

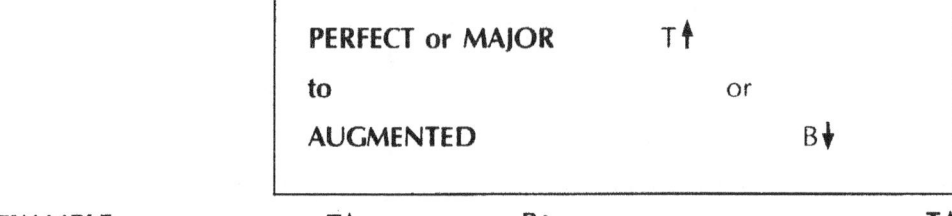

EXAMPLE

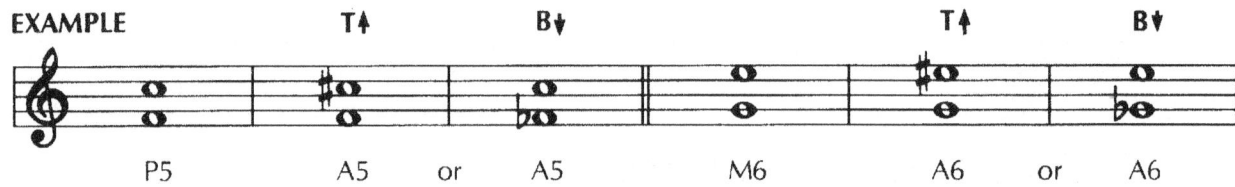

Here is a chart of the relative sizes of all types of interval. The arrows indicate the number of semitones between each type.

EXERCISES

(1) Change these Perfect and Major intervals into Augmented intervals. T↑ or B↓.
Name all the intervals in the spaces below.

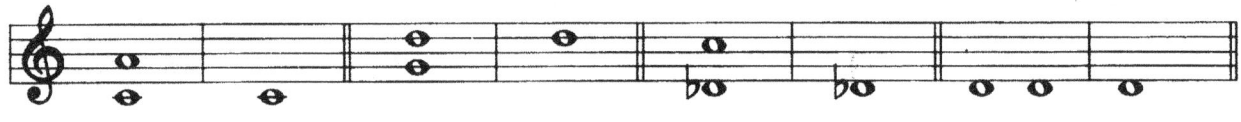

(2) Identify these intervals as Perfect, Major or Augmented Intervals.

(3) Write the following intervals **ABOVE** the given notes.

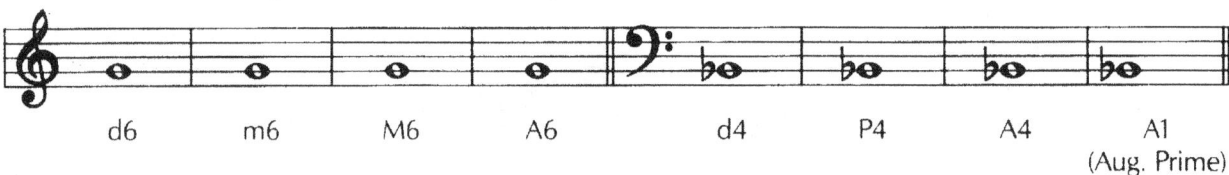

d6   m6   M6   A6   d4   P4   A4   A1
                                    (Aug. Prime)

LESSON TWENTY-SEVEN

INVERSIONS OF INTERVALS

To 'invert' means to **turn upside down**.

To invert an interval take the lower note and raise it an octave, or take the upper note and lower it by an octave.

An easy way to remember what size the original interval becomes when inverted, is to add the numbers of both intervals.

ANY INTERVAL AND ITS INVERSION ADD UP TO THE NUMBER **NINE**

a Prime inverted becomes an 8ve   1 + 8 = 9
a 2nd inverted becomes a 7th   2 + 7 = 9
a 3rd inverted becomes a 6th   3 + 6 = 9
a 4th inverted becomes a 5th   4 + 5 = 9

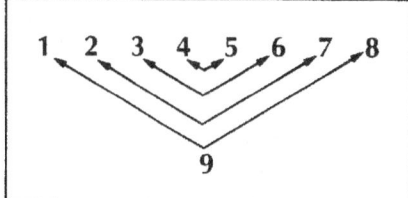

The reverse is true for all of the above.

8 + 1 = 9;   7 + 2 = 9;   6 + 3 = 9;   5 + 4 = 9

THE MIRROR EFFECT

The TYPE OF INTERVAL becomes opposite when inverted.

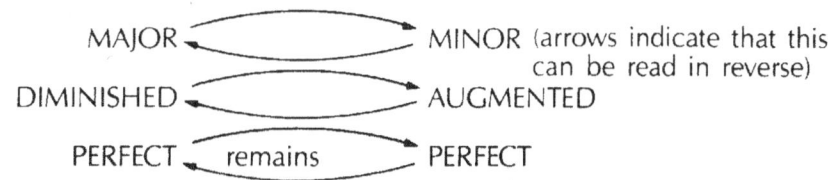

SIZE AND TYPE

Using the above information we find that for example:

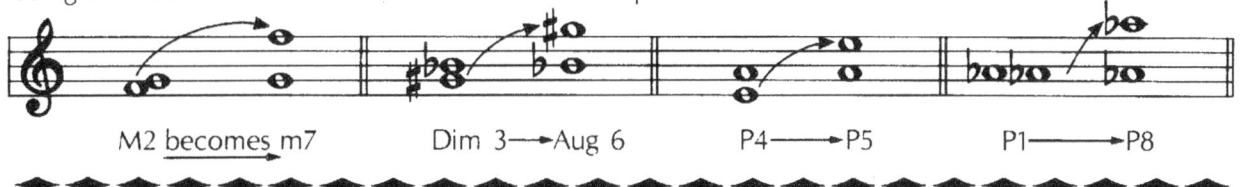

M2 becomes m7   Dim 3 → Aug 6   P4 → P5   P1 → P8

◆◆◆◆◆◆◆◆◆◆◆◆◆◆◆◆◆◆◆◆◆◆◆◆◆◆◆◆◆◆◆◆

EXERCISES

(1) Fill in the blanks

   (a) Diminished is the opposite of ....

   (b) Minor is the opposite of ....

   (c) Perfect intervals when inverted remain ....

   (d) An inverted 6th becomes a .... and an inverted 2nd becomes a ....

(2) Name the given interval, then invert it and name the inversion.

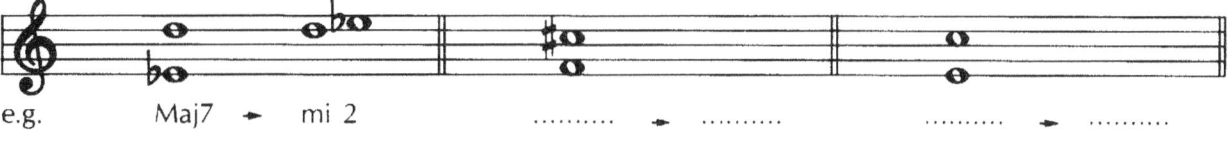

e.g.   Maj7 → mi 2   .... → .... → ....

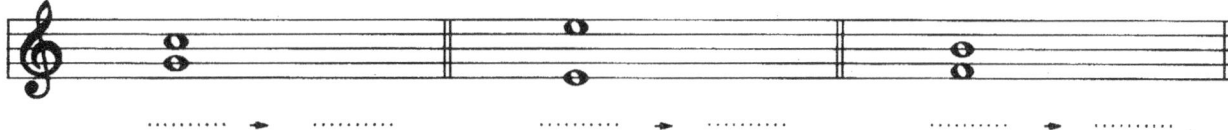

.... → .... → .... → ....

LESSON TWENTY-EIGHT

INTERVAL SOUNDS

All the intervals covered on the previous pages fall into one of three groups according to their sound. These groupings are:

1. The PERFECT SOUNDING intervals: P1, P4, P5, P8

2. The CONSONANT or pleasant sounding intervals: Major and Minor 3rds and 6ths.
   (Consonant means 'sounding together' from 'con' meaning 'with' and 'son' meaning 'sound')

3. The DISSONANT or harsh sounding intervals: Major and Minor 2nds and 7ths and the Augmented 4th or Diminished 5th interval (the Tritone). (Dissonant means 'sounding against' from 'dis' meaning against and 'son' meaning 'sound'.)

*Some textbooks regard groups 1 and 2 as Perfect Consonant and Imperfect Consonant sounds, as both groups have a pleasant sound. The **Perfect Intervals** can be regarded as having an open and clear sound which distinguishes them from the **Consonant Intervals** which have a more blended sound. I have therefore presented them as separate groupings.*

* THE TRITONE — This name has been given to the interval that contains **Three Tones** and can be named also as either the Augmented Fourth or Diminished Fifth. From any note to the Tritone above or below it gives the mid-point of the octave, as the distance of an Octave is **Six Tones**.

INVERSIONS OF INTERVALS

Any interval in each of the three groups will remain in its group even when inverted. (The original quality of sound is not changed simply because one of the notes is altered by an octave.)

TAKE SOME TIME TO PLAY EACH OF THESE INTERVALS ON A KEYBOARD OR ON YOUR FAVOURED INSTRUMENT WHILE LISTENING CLOSELY FOR THE QUALITY OF SOUND.

For further practice in Aural Training in this field refer to my '**Contemporary Aural Course**'.

◆◆◆◆◆◆◆◆◆◆◆◆◆◆◆◆◆◆◆◆◆◆◆

EXERCISES

Complete these sentences

1. Major and Minor 3rds and 6ths are .... intervals.

2. The Dissonant sounding intervals are .... , ... and ....

3. A Perfect sounding interval will sound .... when inverted.

4. The Augmented 4th and Diminished 5th intervals are also known as the ....
   as the distance between the notes is ....

LESSON TWENTY-NINE
UNEVEN OR ODD TIME SIGNATURES

In the folk music of many countries we find music in Time Signatures other than those in the Simple and Compound categories which are all either in Duple, Triple or Quadruple Meters.

In such countries as Roumania, Greece and India music is played in Odd Time Meters which have such upper numbers as 5, 7, 11 or 13. The Beat Note can still be represented by any of the standard note values: i.e. 1/2, 1/4, 1/8 or 1/16th notes. Time signatures could therefore be $\frac{5}{2}$ or $\frac{7}{4}$ or $\frac{11}{8}$ or $\frac{13}{16}$ etc. Two of these Time Signatures (those with 5 or 7 beats per bar) have also become popular with Contemporary Composers and Jazz Composers and musicians.

5 The $\frac{5}{4}$ or $\frac{5}{8}$ Time Signature is usually divided into subgroups of two and three by the use of accents.

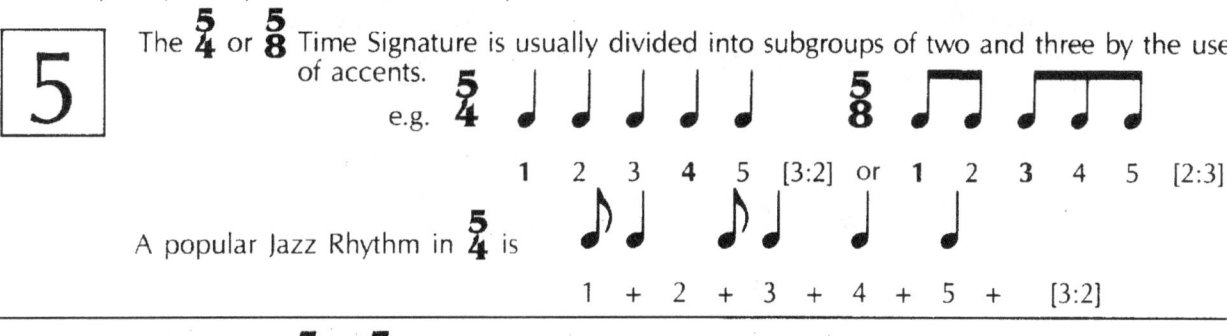

7 Similarly the $\frac{7}{4}$ or $\frac{7}{8}$ Time Signature could be accented:

9 In Greek Music the Time Signatures $\frac{9}{4}$ and $\frac{9}{8}$ may be treated differently to the Compound Time Signatures with 9 as the upper number. The nine pulses are often accented in this manner:

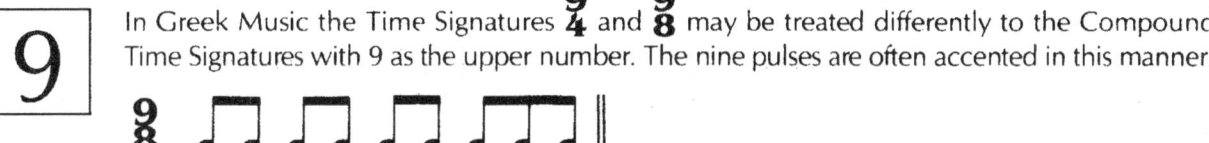

12 Another popular rhythmic variation is the Spanish treatment of twelve pulses in two groups of six each accented differently.
The Time Signature is often written as $\frac{6}{8}\frac{3}{4}$.

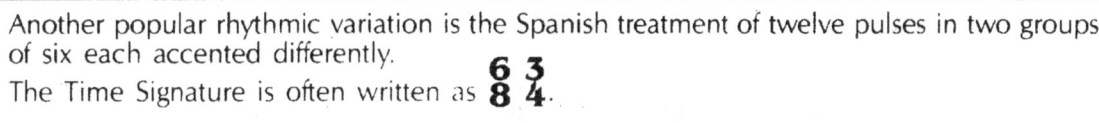

This rhythm is found in Leonard Bernstein's song 'America' from the musical 'West Side Story'.

EXERCISES

(1) Add the bar lines and counting to these lines of music.

(2) Write the Time Signatures for these bars of music and write the counts under the bars.

LESSON THIRTY

REVIEW OF TRIADS

MAJOR AND MINOR TRIADS

The Root Positions of these triads can be found by combining the First, Third and Fifth degrees of the Major and Minor scales respectively.
The Formulas for each chord can be expressed in semitones.
The interval of a Major Third contains 4 semitones.
The interval of a Minor Third contains 3 semitones.

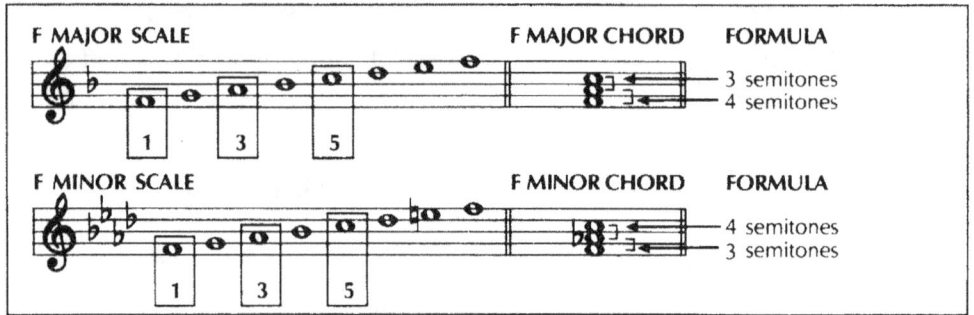

DIMINISHED AND AUGMENTED TRIADS IN ROOT POSITION

These triads can be found by altering notes from the Major Triad or by following the Semitone Formula.

SUSPENDED FOURTH TRIADS IN ROOT POSITION

By replacing the third degree of a Major or Minor triad with the **Fourth** degree of the scale a Suspended Fourth Triad can be formed.

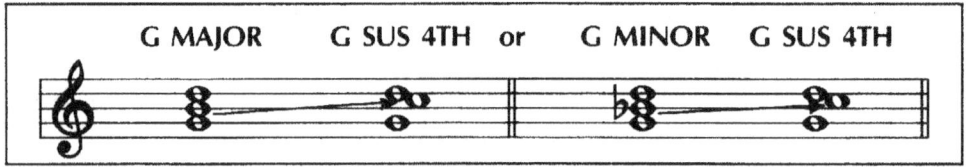

EXERCISES

(1) Indicate the number of semitones in each third and then name each type of triad.

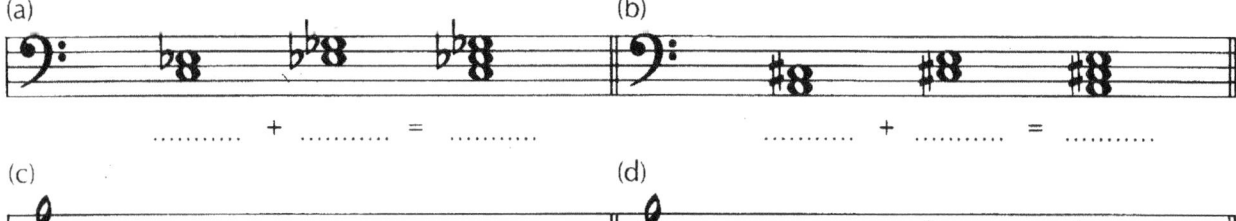

(2) Write these chords in Root Position.

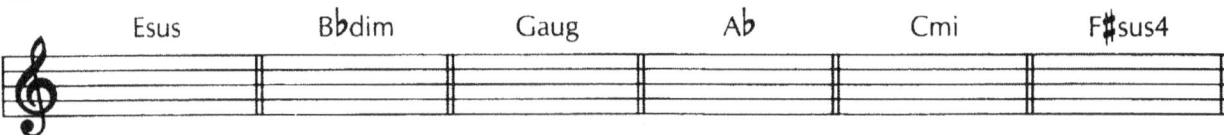

LESSON THIRTY-ONE

MAJOR 7TH, DOMINANT 7TH AND MAJOR 6TH CHORDS

Three of the standard four note chords have a Major Triad at the base of the chord. Each of them has a different interval from the Root Note added to the basic triad.

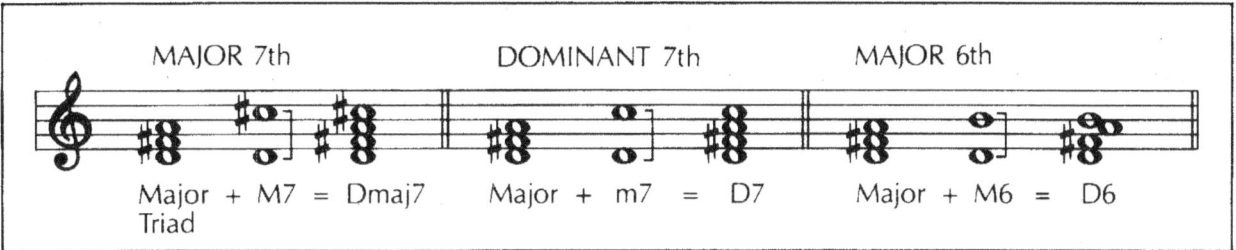

CHORD SYMBOLS

The Modern Chord symbols for these three types of chord are:
maj7 for Major Seventh; **7** for Dominant Seventh; **6** for Major Sixth.
For Example: Dmaj7; D7 and D6

For further approaches to the construction of these chords as well as information as to their positions in the scale and functions, refer to my 'CONTEMPORARY CHORD WORKBOOK' Book 1

EXERCISES

(1) Build Major 7ths, Dominant 7ths and Major 6ths by adding the appropriate intervals to the Major Chords.

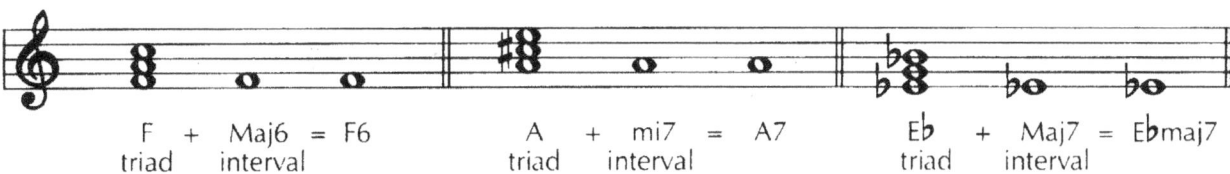

(2) Identify the following chords.

(3) Complete these chords above the given starting notes.

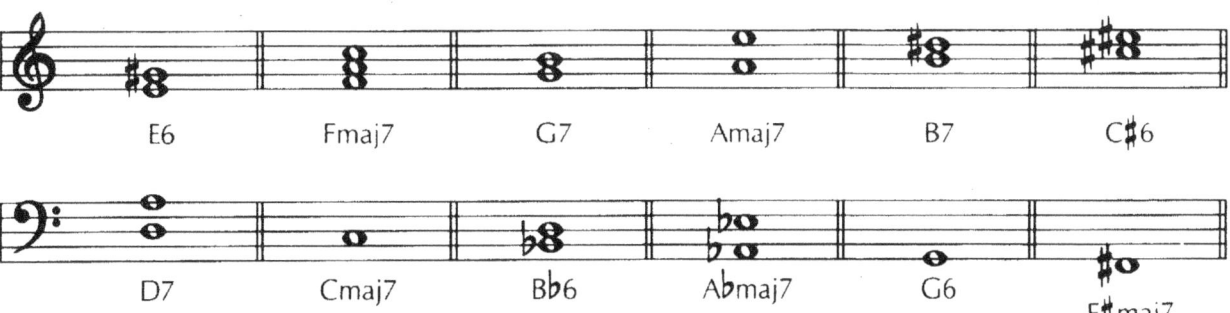

LESSON THIRTY-TWO

MINOR 7TH AND MINOR 6TH CHORDS

The Minor 7th and Minor 6th chords both have a minor triad at the base of the chord. The interval added to the minor triad is a minor 7th interval in the case of the Minor 7th chord and a major 6th interval in the case of the Minor 6th chord.

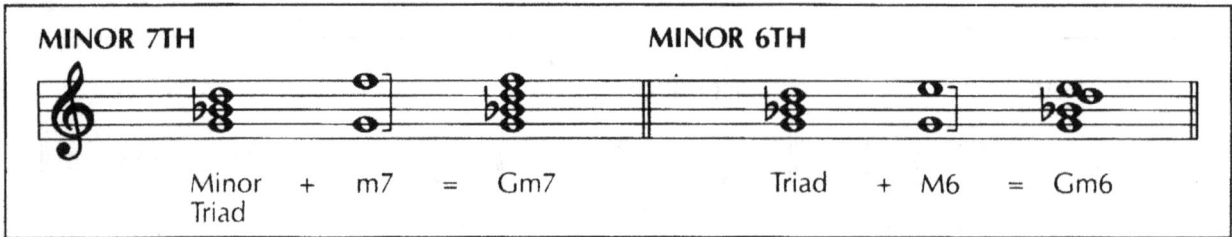

Another means by which you can find the Minor 6th chord is to take a Major 6th chord and lower the third degree.

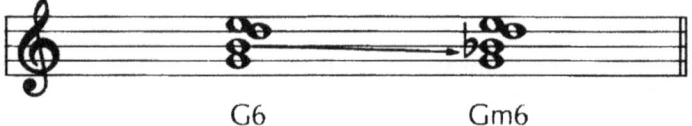

CHORD SYMBOLS

The Modern Chord symbols for these two chords are:
either **m7** or **mi7** for the Minor Seventh chord and
either **m6** or **mi6** for the Minor Sixth chord.
For Example: Dm7 or Dmi7, Dm6 or Dmi6.

◆◆◆◆◆◆◆◆◆◆◆◆◆◆◆◆◆◆◆◆◆◆◆◆◆◆◆◆◆◆◆

EXERCISE

(1) Build Minor 7th and Minor 6th chords by adding the appropriate interval to these minor triads.

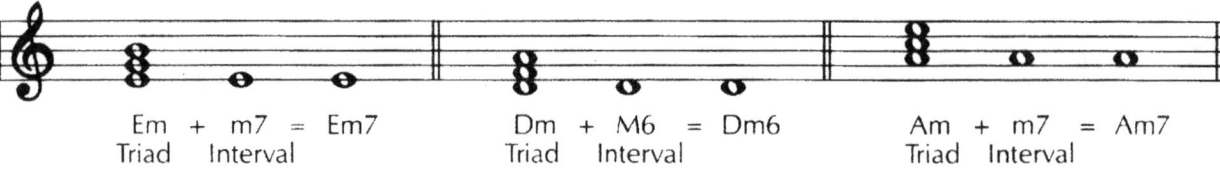

(2) Identify the following chords.

(3) Complete these chords.

Am7   B♭m6   Cm6   Dm6   E♭m7   Gm6

(4) Write these chords above the given starting notes.

Fm7   Em6   Dm7   Cm6   B♭m7   Am6

LESSON THIRTY-THREE

DIMINISHED SEVENTH AND HALF-DIMINISHED SEVENTH CHORDS

The Diminished Seventh and Half-Diminished Seventh chords both have a Diminished Triad at the base of the chord.

The Diminished Seventh chord uses the Diminished Triad with an added **Diminished 7th interval** from the Root Note of the chord.

The Half-Diminished Seventh chord uses the Diminished Triad with an added **Minor 7th interval** from the Root Note of the chord.

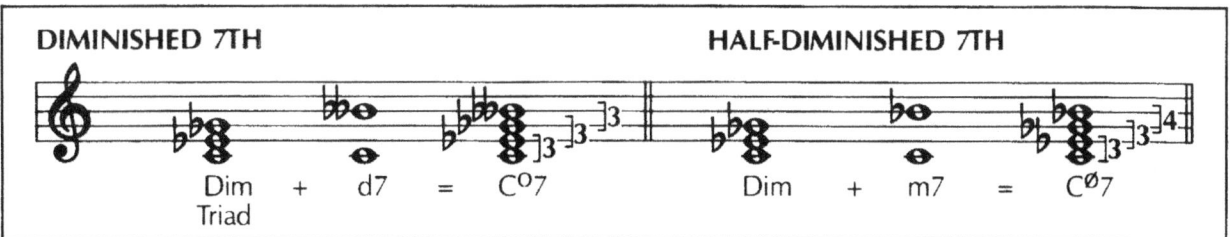

The **formula** in semitones for the **Diminished Seventh** chord is 3. 3. 3.

The **formula** in semitones for the **Half-Diminished Seventh** chord is 3. 3. 4.
(As you can see, not quite the same as a full Dim 7 chord).

CHORD SYMBOLS

The Modern Chord symbol for a Diminished Seventh interval is either the circle (o) as for the Diminished Triad, or the circle with a 7 next to it (o7) or in some cases the short form of the word (dim7)

FOR EXAMPLE. D° or D°7 or Ddim7

The modern Chord symbol for the Half-Diminished Seventh chord is the circle with a diagonal line cutting through it (ø).

MINOR 7♭5

Another name for the Half-Diminished Seventh chord is minor 7th♭5. An alternative way to form this chord is to take a Minor Seventh chord and flatten the 5th degree. The Modern Chord symbol is therefore m7♭5 or mi7♭5 and can be used instead of ø7.

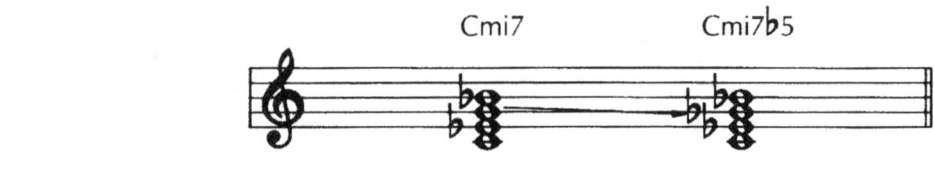

◆◆◆◆◆◆◆◆◆◆◆◆◆◆◆◆◆◆◆◆◆◆◆◆◆◆◆◆◆

EXERCISES

(1) Build full and half-diminished seventh chords by adding the appropriate interval to these Diminished Triads.

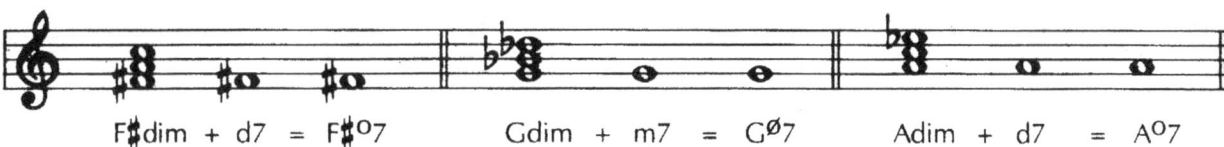

(2) Add accidentals to these chords to agree with the chord symbols. Use either the Semitone Formula or the added interval approach to arrive at the correct chord notation.

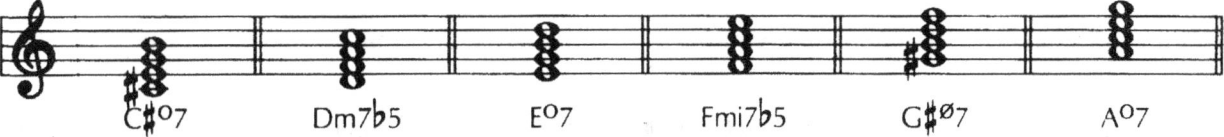

LESSON THIRTY-FOUR

CHORD REVIEW EXERCISES

Below are some review exercises on both three and four-note chord types. For extra practice in these areas plus additional information on the **inversions** of the **four-note chords**, refer to my Contemporary Chord Workbook, Book 1.

(1) Identify the following triads in Root Position.

(2) Write these triads in the inversions called for.

(3) Identify the following four-note chords.

(4) Write the requested four-note chords above the given Root Notes.

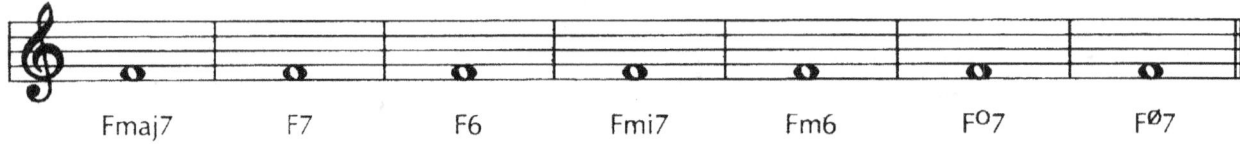

(5) Add accidentals to form the type of four-note required. A clue to this exercise is that only one note needs to be altered in each succeeding chord.

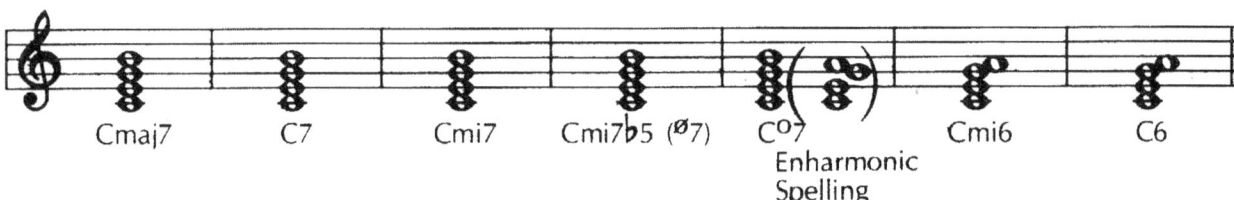

Special Note.

Sometimes Diminished 7th chords are written with Enharmonic Spellings to avoid the use of Double Sharps or Double Flats.

e.g. The correct spelling for Cdim7 is C E♭ G♭ B♭♭ but it is sometimes spelled C E♭ G♭ A or C E♭ F♯ A.

38

LESSON THIRTY-FIVE

TEST YOUR KNOWLEDGE

Fill in the blanks.

(1) Dotted Beat Notes are found in .... Time Signatures.

(2) The Relative Minor Scale is found on the .... note of the Major.

(3) The .... chord and the .... chord both have a minor triad at the base of the four-note chord.

(4) To modulate means to ....

(5) This is the signpost note ....

(6) A group of **two** notes found in a Compound Time signature is called ....

(7) In the .... Minor scale the ascending scale is different to the descending scale.

(8) is the interval of a .... or Compound ....

(9) Three Compound Triple Time-Signatures are .... , ... and ....

(10) The difference between the Key Signatures of the Tonic Major and Tonic Minor keys on A is .... sharps.

(11) is a ....

(12) The types of intervals found between the Tonic Note and any other note of the Major scale are .... and ....

(13) is a .... sign.

(14) The three forms of Minor Scale are the .... , ... and .... minor scales.

(15) A Triplet is a group of .... notes found only in .... Time-Signatures.

(16) The Dissonant Sounding intervals are ....

(17) To find the Relative Major scale to the Tonic note of any minor scale, first go up a .... then up a ....

(18) M.M. stands for ....

(19) The two types of four-note chord which have a Diminished Triad at the base of the chord are the .... and the ....

(20) Uneven Time-Signatures may have .... , ... , ... or .... as the top number.

(21) The term 'minor' when applied to intervals means ....

(22) To convert a Natural Minor scale to the Harmonic form the .... degree must be .... by a semitone.

(23) The three types of four-note chords which have a Major Triad at the base of the triad are the .... , ... and ....

(24) When a Major Interval has the upper note raised by a semitone it becomes an .... interval.

(25) Dal Segno (D.S.) al Fine means ....
....

(26) The Modulation points for the key of D Major are:

....	2♯'s	....
....	D	....
....	....	....

ANSWER SHEET

ANSWER SHEET

ANSWER SHEET

Lesson Thirty: Q.1 (a) m3 + m3 = dim (b) M3 + m3 = Maj (c) m3 + M3 = min
(d) M3 + M3 = Aug

Lesson Thirty-One: Q.1

+ = F6   + = A7   + = Ebmaj7

Q.2 Cmaj7   C6,   C7,   G6,   G7   Gmaj7
Q.3

Lesson Thirty-Two: Q.1

+ = Em7   + = Dm6   + = Am7

Q.2 Bbm7, C#m6, Fm6, Bm7, Dm7, F#m6
Q.3

Q.4

Lesson Thirty-Three: Q.1

+ = F#o7   + = Gø7   + = Ao7

Q.2

Lesson Thirty-Four: Q.1 Adim, A, A Aug, Bbsus4, Bbm, Bb Aug
Q.2

Q.3 Em7, F6, G half-dim7 or Gm7b5, Am6, Bbmaj7, C# half-dim7, D7
Q.4

Q.5

Lesson Thirty-Five: (1) Compound (2) 6th (3) Minor 6th and Minor 7th (4) change key
(5) Very High C (6) Duplet (7) Melodic (8) 9th, Compound 2nd
(9) $\frac{9}{4}, \frac{9}{8}, \frac{9}{16}$ (10) three (11) Demisemiquaver, 32nd note
(12) Perfect, Major (13) Coda (14) Natural, Harmonic and Melodic
(15) Three, Simple (16) 2nds, 7ths, Tritone (17) Tone, Semitone
(18) Maelzel's Metronome (19) Dim7 and Half-Dim7 or mi7b5
(20) 5, 7, 9, 11 (21) lesser (22) 7th, raised
(23) Major 7th, Major 6th, Dominant 7th (24) Augmented (25) Return to
the Sign and then play until the end or where the word 'Fine' appears

G	D	A
Em	Bm	F#m

LESSON ONE

THE MODES

Music prior to the Seventeenth Century was written and played in several scales known as MODES. As the written forms of these scales were mostly notated by the monks and used in Church settings, they became known as Ecclesiastical or Church Modes.

Two of these Modes are already known to you as the Major and Natural Minor scales. They are the **Ionian** and **Aeolian** Modes respectively.

Each of the Modes can be represented by a white note scale on a keyboard. The different sounds of each Mode are the result of varying arrangements of the Tones and Semitones.

All Modes can be TRANSPOSED to any of the twelve notes of the Octave.

The names of the Modes were taken from names given to the Ancient Greek Modes. Each of the Greek Modes was given a name related to a region or tribe of Ancient Greece: Doria, Phrygia, Lydia and so on. The later Church Modes however had no connection with the Early Greek Modes other than the borrowed names.

THE MODES

The **semitones** in each Mode are marked by a **slur.**

LESSON TWO

MODAL SOUNDS

The seven Church Modes each have a different tone colour depending upon whether they are closer to the Major or Minor Scale in sound.

> There are: - Three Major-sounding Modes.
> - Three Minor-sounding Modes.
> - One Mode which sounds half way between Major and minor and is therefore known as the Mode of **Median Stability**.

Each Mode in the example below has been transposed so that the starting note in each case is C. This has been done so that you can easily compare each Mode to C major scale (Ionian Mode). You will notice that the more lowered notes in each Mode the darker the tone colour of the Mode

The example presents the Modes in order of brightness or darkness.

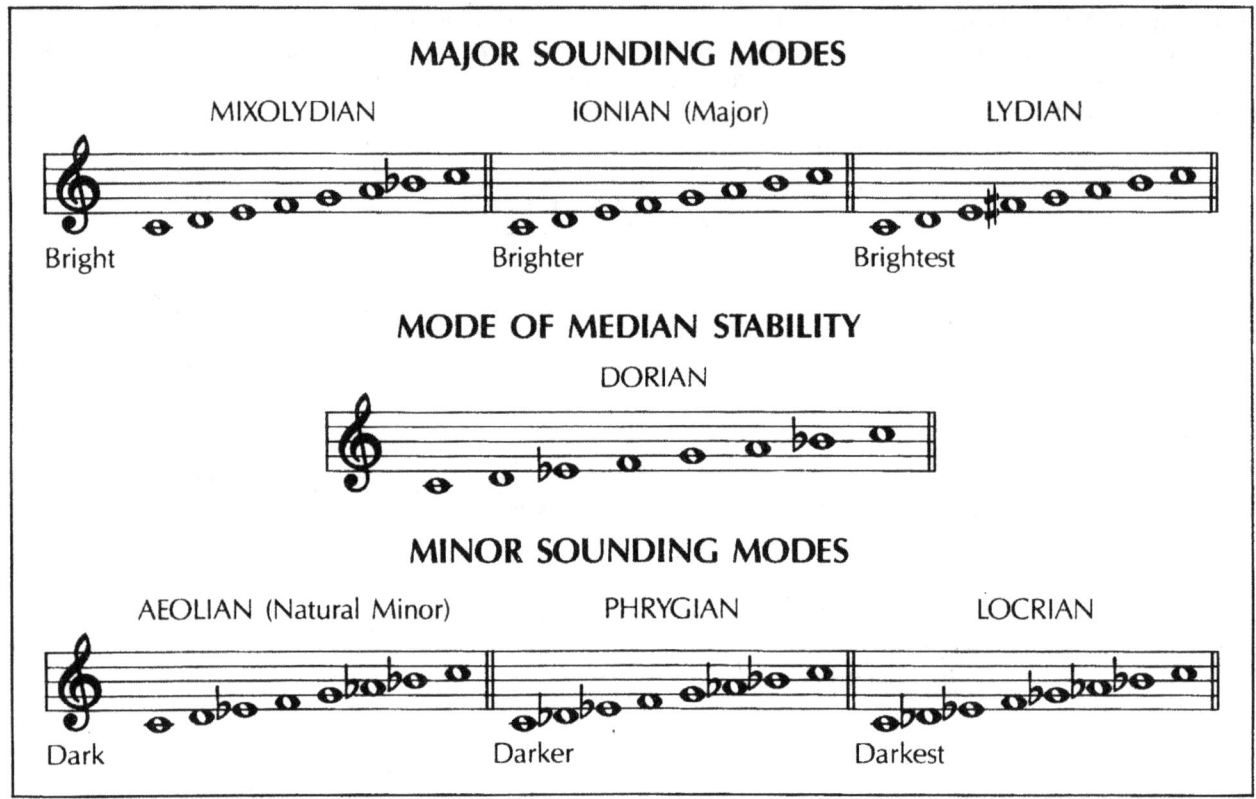

◆◆◆◆◆◆◆◆◆◆◆◆◆◆◆◆◆◆◆◆◆◆◆◆◆◆◆◆◆

EXERCISES

Complete these sentences:

(1) The brightest of the Major sounding Modes is the .... Mode.

(2) The Dorian Mode is known as the Mode of ....

(3) The darkest sounding Mode is the ....

(4) The Major scale is also known as the .... Mode.

(5) Another name for the Aeolian Mode is .... scale.

On the following pages each Mode will be approached from two points of view; either comparing the Mode to the Major scale on the same starting note or regarding the Mode as simply the notes of another Major scale played over a different range, that is: from the second note to the octave above or from the third note of the scale to the octave above. etc.

LESSON THREE

THE DORIAN MODE

APPROACH ONE
A formula for finding the Dorian Mode can be worked out when the Dorian Mode on D is compared to the Major Scale in D.

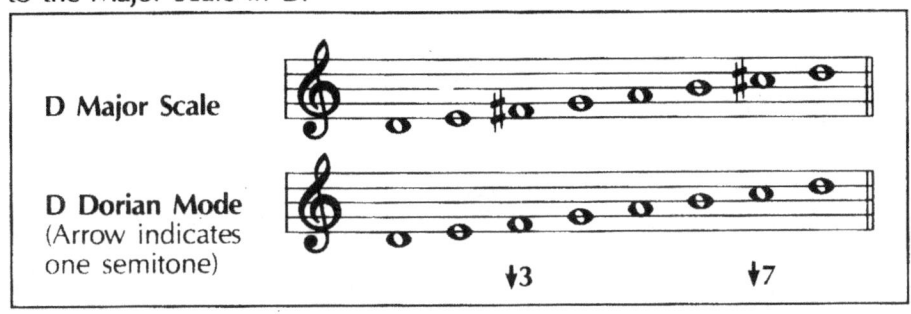

APPROACH TWO
The Dorian Mode on D can be thought of as C Major Scale played from the 2nd note to the Octave above.

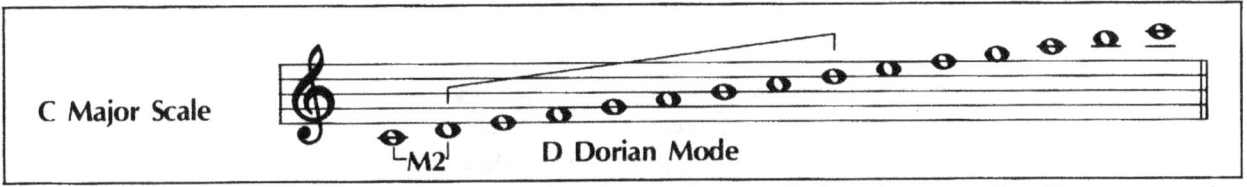

By comparing the two scales, one can see that the Dorian Mode has the same Key Signature as the Major Scale that is a **Major Second** lower than the keynote of the Mode.

CHORDS DERIVED FROM THE DORIAN MODE — MINOR 7TH, MINOR 6TH
Two types of four-note chords can be found by combining notes above the Tonic Note of the Dorian scale. They are the Minor 7th and Minor 6th chords. (1, 3, 5, 7 and 1, 3, 5, 6). When either of these types of chords are found in music therefore, the Dorian Scale played against these chords will blend perfectly.

EXERCISES

(1) Lower the 3rd and 7th degrees of the following Major Scales to create Dorian Modes. Then combine the 1st, 3rd, 5th & 7th degrees or the 1st, 3rd, 5th and 6th degrees to build Minor 7th and Minor 6th chords on the Tonic Notes of the Modes.

(2) Write these Dorian Modes using Approach One, then indicate which Major Scales have the same Key Signature as the Modes.

G Dorian = [ ] Major Scale   B Dorian = [ ] Major Scale

(3) First find the number of sharps or flats in the Key Signature of the Major scale which is a **Major Second** lower than the starting note of each of these Modes. Next add those accidentals to the given scale in order to form Dorian Modes.

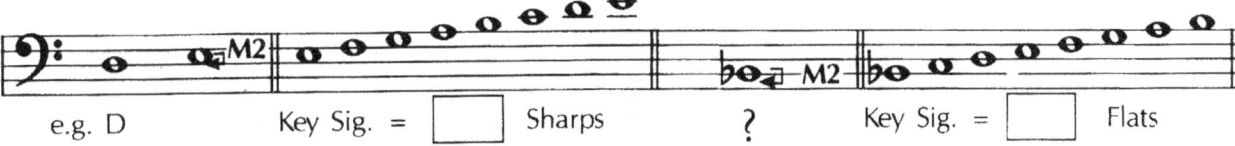

e.g. D   Key Sig. = [ ] Sharps   ?   Key Sig. = [ ] Flats

LESSON FOUR

THE PHRYGIAN MODE

APPROACH ONE
A formula for finding the Phrygian Mode can be worked out by comparing the Phrygian Mode on E to the Major Scale on E.

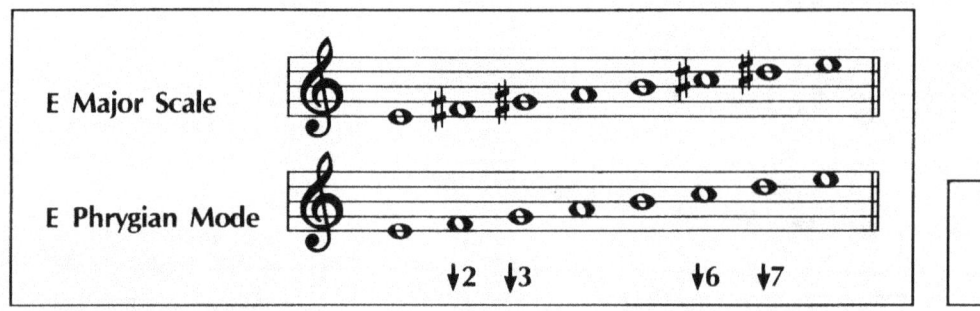

APPROACH TWO
The Phrygian Mode on E can be thought of as C Major Scale played from the 3rd note to the Octave above.

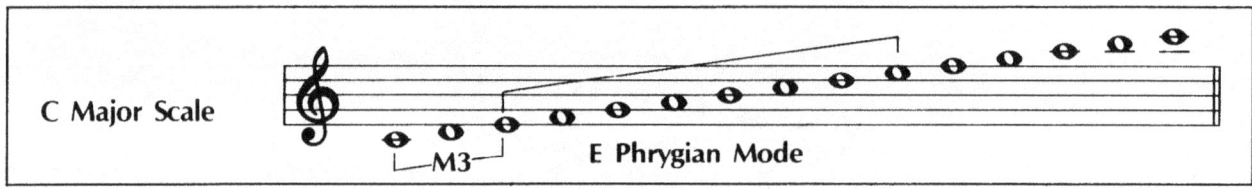

By comparing the two scales, one can see that the Phrygian Mode has the same Key Signature as the Major Scale that is a **Major Third** lower than the keynote of the Mode.

CHORD DERIVED FROM THE PHRYGIAN MODE — MINOR 7TH
If the 1st, 3rd, 5th and 7th notes of the Phrygian Mode are combined, the resulting chord is a **Minor 7th** chord. The Phrygian Mode can therefore be played over any Minor 7th chord. However the **Tone Colour** of this Mode will be darker than that of the Dorian Mode and as a result the Phrygian Mode is usually only used when that particular effect is desired. (The Dorian Mode remains the first choice when choosing a scale to cover the Minor 7th chord.)

EXERCISES

(1) Lower the 2nd, 3rd, 6th and 7th degrees of these Major Scales to create Phrygian Modes. Then write the 7th chord built on the Tonic Notes of the Mode.

(2) Write these Phrygian Modes using Approach One, then indicate which Major Scales have the same Key Signature as the Modes.

A Phrygian = [ ] Major Scale   F Phrygian = [ ] Major Scale

(3) First find out the Key Signature of the Major scale a **Major Third** lower than the starting notes of these Modes, then add those accidentals to the given scale in order to form Phrygian Modes.

LESSON FIVE

THE LYDIAN MODE

APPROACH ONE
A formula for finding the Lydian Mode can be worked out by comparing the Lydian Mode on F to the Major Scale on F.

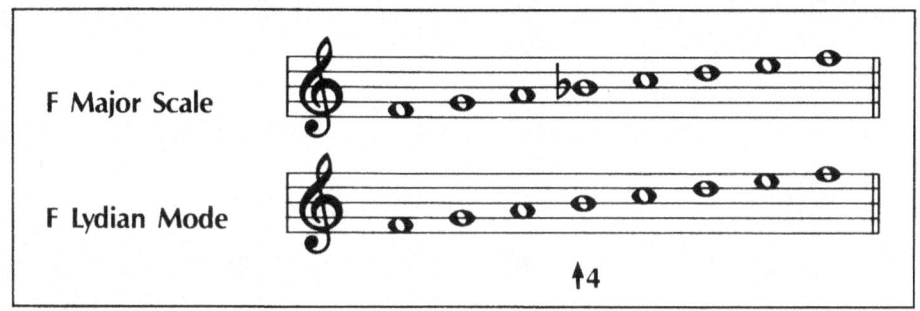

APPROACH TWO
The Lydian Mode on F can be thought of as C Major Scale played from the 4th note to the Octave above.

By comparing the two scales, one can see that the Lydian Mode has the same Key Signature as the Major Scale that is a **Perfect Fourth** lower than the keynote of the Mode.

CHORDS DERIVED FROM THE LYDIAN MODE — MAJOR 7TH, MAJOR 6TH
Two types of four-note chords can be found by combining notes above the Tonic Note of the Lydian Mode. They are the **Major 7th** and **Major 6th** chords. When the Lydian Mode is played over these types of chords a bright tone colour is created.

◆◆◆◆◆◆◆◆◆◆◆◆◆◆◆◆◆◆◆◆◆◆◆

EXERCISES

(1) Raise the 4th degree of these Major Scales to create Lydian Modes. Then combine the 1st, 3rd, 5th and 7th, or 1st, 3rd, 5th and 6th degrees to build Major 7th and Major 6th chords on the Tonic Notes of the Modes.

(2) Write these Lydian Modes using Approach One, then indicate which Major Scales have the same Key Signature as the Modes.

B♭ Lydian = [ ] Major Scale   E Lydian = [ ] Major Scale

(3) First find the number of sharps or flats in the Key Signature of the Major scale a **Perfect Fourth** lower than the starting notes of these Modes. Next add those accidentals to the given scale in order to form Lydian Modes.

LESSON SIX

THE MIXOLYDIAN MODE

APPROACH ONE
A formula for finding the Mixolydian Mode can be worked out by comparing the Mixolydian Mode on G to the Major Scale on G.

APPROACH TWO
The Mixolydian Mode on G can be thought of as C Major Scale played from the 5th note to the Octave above.

By comparing the two scales, one can see that the Mixolydian Mode has the same Key Signature as the Major Scale that is a **Perfect Fifth** lower than the keynote of the Mode.

CHORDS DERIVED FROM THE MIXOLYDIAN MODE — DOMINANT 7TH, MAJOR 6TH
Two types of four-note chords can be found by combining notes above the Tonic Note of the Mixolydian Mode. They are the Dominant 7th and Major 6th chords. The Mode is most frequently used with the Dominant 7th chord.

◆◆◆◆◆◆◆◆◆◆◆◆◆◆◆◆◆◆◆◆◆◆◆◆◆◆◆◆◆◆◆

EXERCISES

(1) Lower the 7th degrees of these Major Scales to create Mixolydian Modes. Then combine the 1st, 3rd, 5th and 7th, or the 1st, 3rd, 5th and 6th degrees to build Dominant 7th and Major 6th chords on the Tonic Notes of the Modes.

(2) Write these Mixolydian Modes using Approach One, then indicate which Major Scales have the same Key Signature as the Modes.

A Mixolydian = ☐ Major Scale   F Mixolydian = ☐ Major Scale

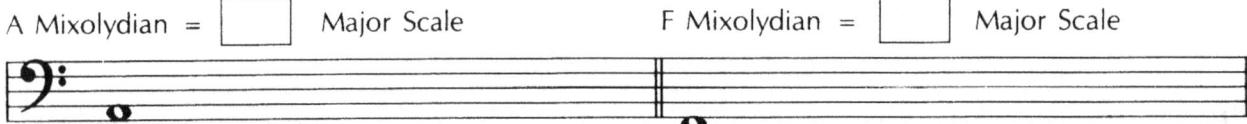

(3) First find the number of sharps or flats in the Key Signature of the Major scale which is a **Perfect Fifth** lower than the starting notes of these Modes. Next add those accidentals to the given scale in order to form Mixolydian Modes.

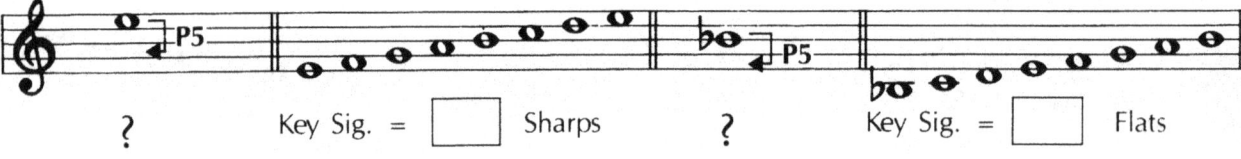

?   Key Sig. = ☐ Sharps   ?   Key Sig. = ☐ Flats

LESSON SEVEN

THE AEOLIAN MODE

APPROACH ONE
A formula for finding the Aeolian Mode can be worked out by comparing the Aeolian Mode on A to the Major Scale in A.

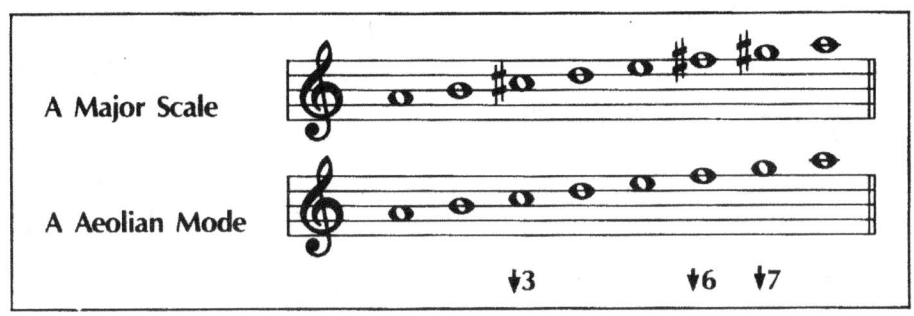

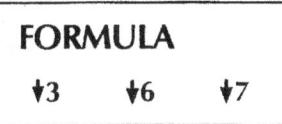

APPROACH TWO
The Aeolian Mode on A can be thought of as C Major Scale played from the 6th note to the Octave above.

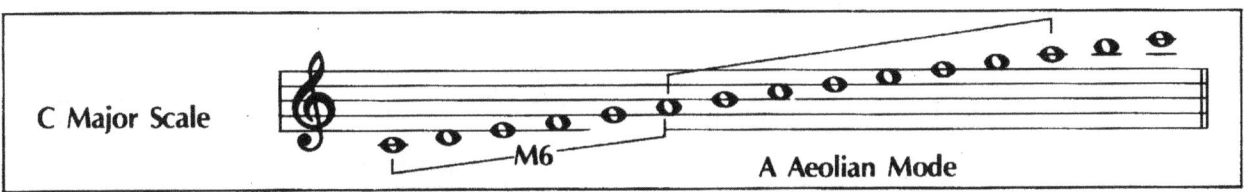

By comparing the two scales, one can see that the Aeolian Mode has the same Key Signature as the Major Scale that is a **Major Sixth** lower than the keynote of the Mode. (Remember that the Aeolian Mode is in fact the Natural Minor Scale that was discussed in Book 3 of this series.)

CHORD DERIVED FROM THE AEOLIAN MODE — MINOR 7TH
By combining the 1st, 3rd, 5th and 7th notes of this Mode a **Minor 7th** chord can be created. The Aeolian Mode is slightly darker in tone colour than the Dorian Mode when played against the Minor 7th chord.

EXERCISES

(1) Lower the 3rd, 6th and 7th degrees of these Major Scales to create Aeolian Modes. Then combine the 1st, 3rd, 5th and 7th degrees to build Minor 7th chords on the Tonic Notes of the Modes.

(2) Write these Aeolian Modes using Approach One, then indicate which Major Scales have the same Key Signature as the Modes.

B Aeolian Mode = [ ] Major Scale   D Aeolian Mode = [ ] Major Scale

(3) First find the number of sharps or flats in the Key Sign of the Major Scale that is a **Major Sixth** lower (or a Minor 3rd higher) than the starting notes of these Modes. Next add those accidentals to the given scale in order to form Aeolian Modes.

?   Key Sig. = [ ] Flats   ?   Key Sig. = [ ] Sharps

LESSON EIGHT

THE LOCRIAN MODE

APPROACH ONE
A formula for finding the Locrian Mode can be worked out by comparing the Locrian Mode on B to the Major Scale on B.

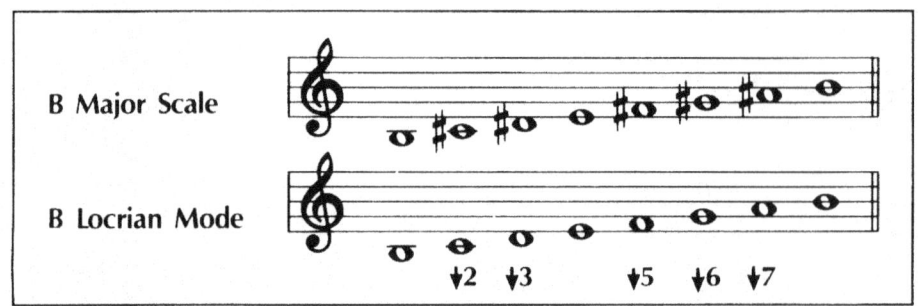

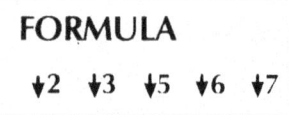

APPROACH TWO
The Locrian Mode on B can be thought of as C Major Scale played from the 7th note to the Octave above.

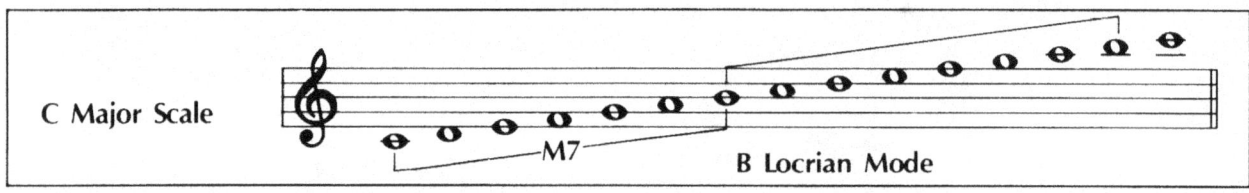

By comparing the two scales, one can see that the Locrian Mode has the same Key Signature as the Major Scale that is a **Major Seventh** lower (or a Minor 2nd higher) than the keynote of the Mode.

CHORDS DERIVED FROM THE LOCRIAN MODE — MINOR 7TH ♭5 OR HALF-DIMINISHED 7TH
When the 1st, 3rd, 5th and 7th degrees of this Mode are combined the resulting chord is a Minor 7th Flattened 5th chord which is also known as the Half-Diminished 7th chord.

EXERCISES

(1) Lower the 2nd, 3rd, 5th 6th and 7th degrees of these Major Scales to create Locrian Modes. Then combine the 1st, 3rd, 5th and 7th degrees to build mi7♭5 or half-diminished 7th (ø) chords.

(2) Write these Locrian Modes using Approach One, then indicate which Major Scales have the same Key Signature as the Modes.

G Locrian Mode = [ ] Major Scale   C♯ Locrian Mode = [ ] Major Scale

(3) First find the number of sharps or flats in the Key Sign of the Major Scale that is a **Major Seventh** lower (or a Minor 2nd higher) than the starting notes of these Modes. Next add those accidentals to the given scale in order to form Locrian Modes.

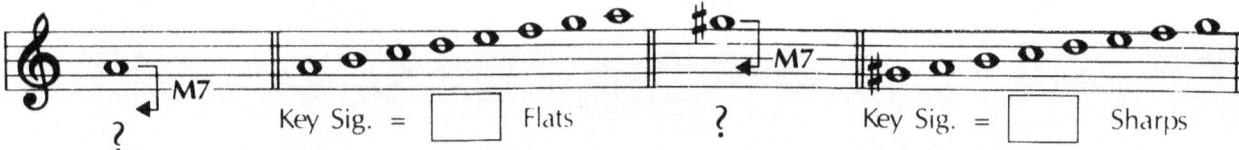

LESSON NINE
MODES IN REVIEW
EXERCISES

(1) Fill in the blanks.
  (a) When the 3rd and 7th degrees of a Major scale are lowered a .... Mode is formed.
  (b) The Mode which best suits the Dominant 7th chord is the .... Mode.
  (c) The brightest sounding Mode is the .... Mode.
  (d) The Locrian Mode is best suited to the .... chord.

(2) Write these Modes on the starting notes given.

Phrygian   Lydian

Dorian   Locrian

(3) Identify the following Modes.

(a)   (b)

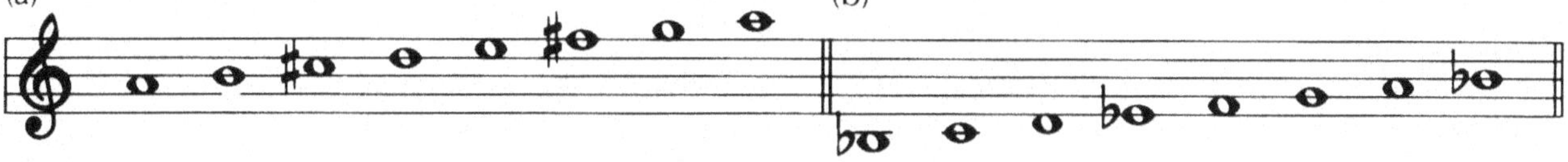

(c)   (d)

(4) Write and name three Modes all beginning on the same note to suit the given chord.

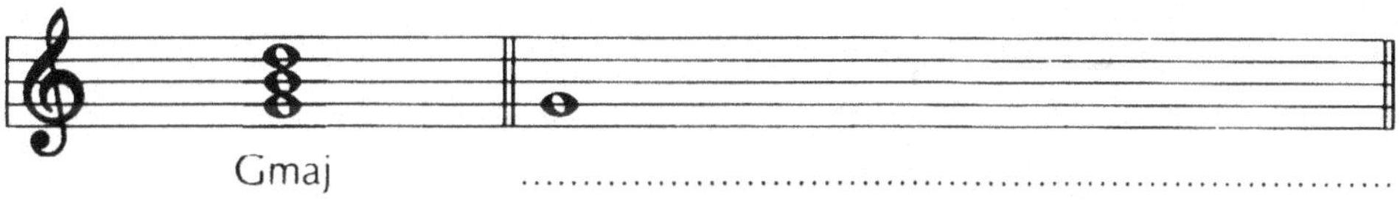

Gmaj

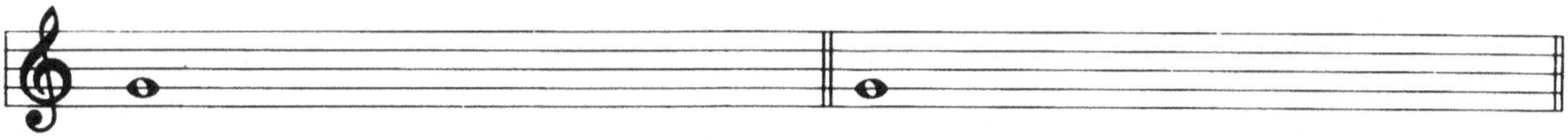

(5) Write and name another three Modes all beginning on the same note to suit this given chord.

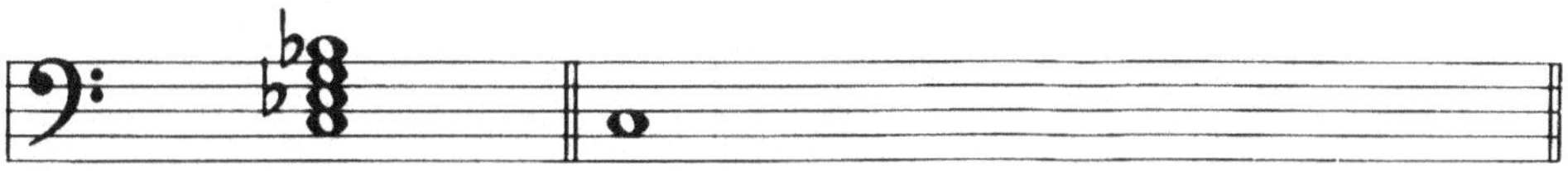

Cm7

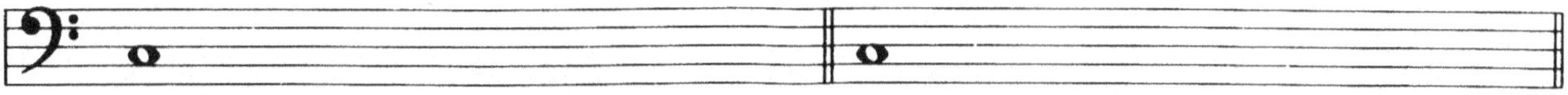

LESSON TEN

SINGLE, DOUBLE AND TRIPLE DOTTED NOTES AND RESTS

As seen in Book 1 of this series, notes can be increased in length by placing dots after the notes.

SINGLE DOTS
By placing a single dot after a note, the note is lengthened by HALF of its original value.

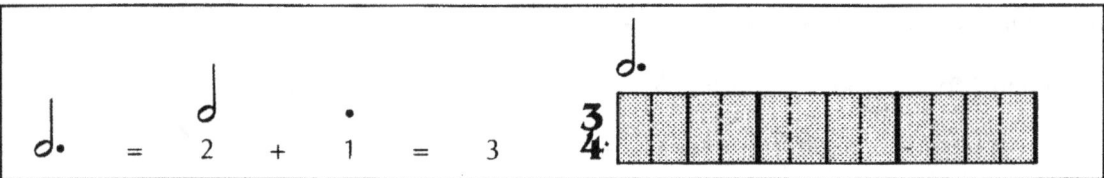

DOUBLE DOTS
If a second dot is placed behind the note, the note is said to be Double Dotted. The second dot adds a QUARTER of the value of the original note (half of the half) to the combined value.

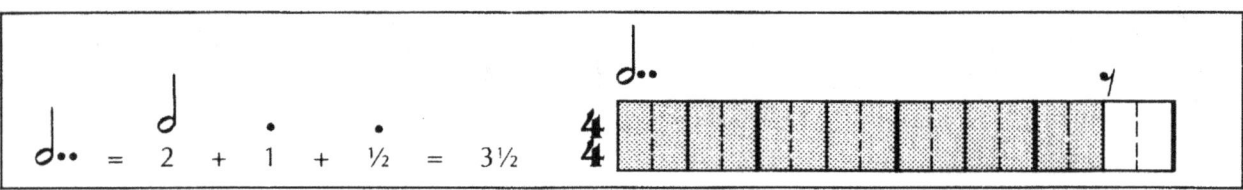

TRIPLE DOTS
If a third dot is placed behind the note the note is said to be Triple Dotted. The third dot adds an EIGHTH of the original value of the note to the combined value. (half of the quarter.)

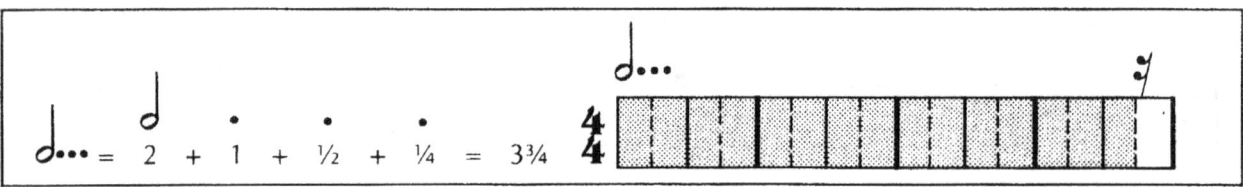

DOTTED RESTS
Exactly the same process can be applied to rests.

EXERCISES

(1) Rewrite these dotted notes and rests using notes and rests tied to each other.

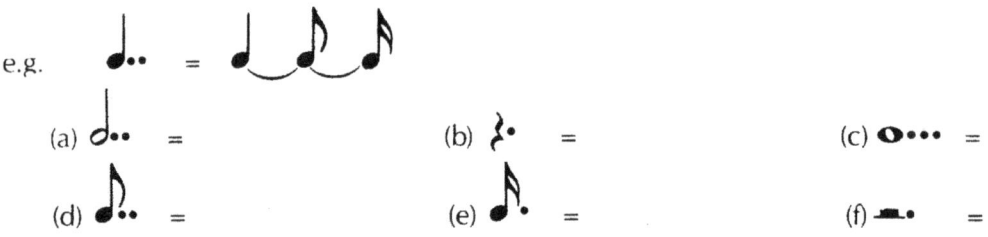

(2) Complete these bars of music using Single, Double and Triple dotted notes.

LESSON ELEVEN

SYNCOPATION

Syncopation can be defined as the deliberate upsetting of the natural accents.

NATURAL ACCENTS

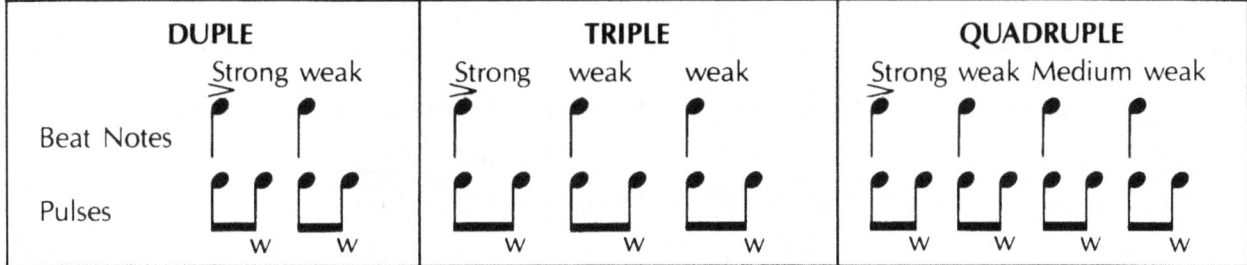

To create a syncopated effect in any of the above meters, several methods can be used.

1. **RESTS** Place a rest where a strong beat should be.
2. **TIES** Tie the previous note over so that a strong beat is not struck.
3. **ACCENTS** Place an accent on a weaker beat or pulse.
4. **MORE TIME VALUE** Combine the weaker beat notes or pulses so as to give them more time value.

EXAMPLE

Syncopation adds spice and interest to most music and can be found in classical, folk, pop, jazz and contemporary music. It is especially noticeable in music with a Latin American flavour.

EXERCISES

(1) Circle the areas in this piece of music where the Syncopation occurs. N.B. Rests on **weak** beats or pulses do **not** indicate syncopation.

(2) Rewrite this music adding syncopation in the four ways learned above.

LESSON TWELVE

TRIAD REVIEW AND TRIADS FOUND IN MAJOR KEYS

Here are the five types of triad discussed in Part B of Book 1 and Part A of this book. The formula of each triad expressed in Semitones is given below each chord.

MAJOR	MINOR	DIMINISHED	AUGMENTED	SUSPENDED 4TH
3	4	3	4	2
4	3	3	4	5

In all exercises on the following pages, use Upper Case Roman Numerals for Major and Augmented triads and Lower Case Roman Numerals for Minor and Diminished Triads.

EXAMPLE — UPPER CASE: I   II   III   IV   V   VI   VII   VIII

— LOWER CASE: i   ii   iii   iv   v   vi   vii   viii

EXERCISES

(1) Identify the types of triads found on each degree of the Major Scale given below.

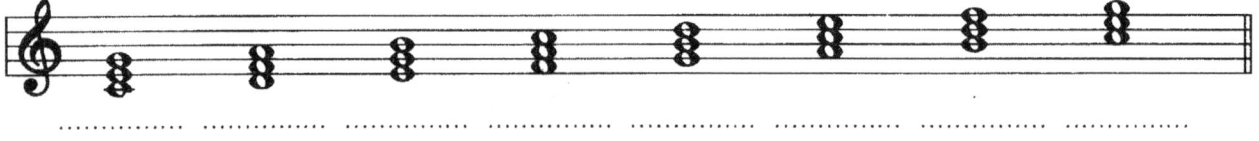

....

(2) Indicate the degrees on which Major Triads occured in Question 1.

....

(3) Indicate the degrees on which the Minor triads occured in Question 1.

....

(4) On which degree of the scale in Question 1 did the Diminished Triad occur? ....

LESSON THIRTEEN

THE MAJOR CHORD TABLE

The information that you will have discovered in completing the questions on the previous page, can be organised into a CHORD TABLE which displays the chords so that one can see the relationship of all the chords to one another.

On the **upper row** of the chord table, the PRIMARY or most important chords are laid out following the sequence found in the CYCLE of FIFTHS.

The **Subdominant** Chord is placed to the Left of the Tonic (representing a Fifth below) while the **Dominant** Chord is placed to the Right of the Tonic Chord (representing a Fifth above).

IV	I	V
F	C	G
ii	vi	iii
Dm	Am	Em
		vii
		B°

On the **second horizontal row** of the Chord Table, the SECONDARY or less important chords are laid out so that the Relative Minor chords are placed directly under their respective Relative Majors.

On the **third row** the only Diminished Triad, found on the Seventh Degree of the Major Scale, is placed directly under the Dominant (Vth) and Mediant (IIIrd) degrees. This is done so that one can see that the chord may easily be used in place of (substituted for) the Dominant Triad.

In a similar fashion each of the Minor Triads could be substituted for the Major Triad in the upper row which is directly above it. The reason for this is, as you will find if you compare the two chords which occur directly above one another, that there is only one note different between each pair of chords.

Placing the chords of each key in the manner shown to form a CHORD TABLE will help you in writing Harmony and when analysing the chords in a piece of music.

◆◆◆◆◆◆◆◆◆◆◆◆◆◆◆◆◆◆◆◆◆◆

EXERCISES

(1) Write the Scale of D Major using a Key Signature and place triads above each note. Next, name each triad and arrange the chords to form a CHORD TABLE.

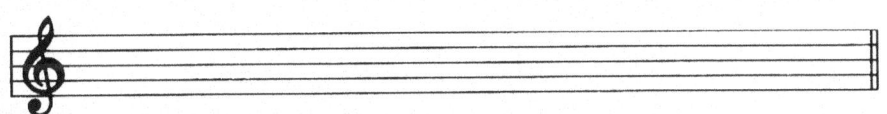

IV	I	V
ii	vi	iii
		vii

(2) Write the Scale of A♭ Major using accidentals and place triads above each note. Name each triad and arrange the chords to form a CHORD TABLE.

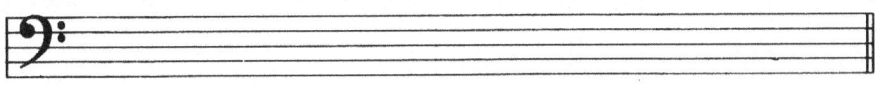

LESSON FOURTEEN

TRIADS FOUND IN MINOR KEYS

Presented below are the three types of Minor Scale, each with the scale-tone chords built above each note.

NATURAL MINOR (Ascending — same as Melodic Minor descending)

HARMONIC MINOR

MELODIC MINOR (Ascending)

EXERCISES

(1) Name each chord in the scales above in the spaces provided below each chord.

(2) Answer the following questions. Remember to use Upper Case Roman Numerals for Major and Augmented and Lower Case Roman Numerals for Minor and Diminished Chords.

On which degrees are the Minor Triads found in the Natural Minor. ____ ____ ____

On which degrees are the Major Triads found in the Natural Minor. ____ ____ ____

On which degree is the Dim. Triad found in the Natural Minor. ____

On which degrees are the Minor Triads found in the Harmonic Minor. ____ ____

On which degrees are the Major Triads found in the Harmonic Minor. ____ ____

On which degrees are the Dim. Triads found in the Harmonic Minor. ____ ____

On which degree is the Aug. Triad found in the Harmonic Minor. ____

In the ascending form only (the descending form is the same as the Natural Minor):

On which degrees are the Minor Triads found in the Melodic Minor. ____ ____

On which degrees are the Major Triads found in the Melodic Minor. ____ ____

On which degrees are the Dim. Triads found in the Melodic Minor. ____ ____

On which degree is the Aug. Triad found in the Melodic Minor. ____

LESSON FIFTEEN
THE MINOR CHORD-TABLE

Now that you have completed Lesson Fourteen, you will have discovered that there are several choices of chord on many of the degrees of the Minor Scale, dependent upon the **form** of the scale employed.

The CHORD TABLE IN A MINOR KEY contains the most **frequently** used chord choices. However, you must keep in mind that any of the chord choices may occur, even if they are not included in the standard table.

On the **upper row,** the PRIMARY CHORDS are placed in the same manner as in the Major Chord Table. However, this time chords i and iv are Minor Chords.

iv	i	V
Fmi	Cmi	G
VI	III(+)	ii°
A♭	E♭(+)	D°
		vii
		B°

The SECONDARY CHORDS in a Minor Chord Table are Chords VI and III which are most frequently MAJOR Chords and Chord ii which is most frequently a Diminished Chord. Chord III has a plus sign in brackets after it, which indicates that it quite often appears as an Augmented Chord. Keep in mind that when the Ascending Melodic Minor Scale is being used in a Melody line, Chord ii often appears as a **Minor Chord** rather than the Diminished chord in the harmonisation.

On the **Third Row**, the diminished triad on chord vii appears, for the same reasons as its appearance in the Major Table.

When working out the names of the notes in a particular key, for the Minor Table, use the Harmonic Minor Scale notes. If you study the example above, you will see that the names for each chord are taken from C Harmonic Minor Scale. (C, D, E♭, F, G, A♭, B, C.) If you learn the position of the degree numbers, you need only move up the scale from 1 to 8 placing the appropriate note name under the correct degree. Note also that in a Minor Table, the two Relative Major keys appear directly under their Relative Minors. Also the three chords which appear in the third vertical row can each be used as **leading function** chords, leading to the Tonic of the Key. (G, D° and B°.)

EXERCISES

(1) Write the Scale of G Harmonic Minor, then complete the chord table for the Key.

iv	i	V
VI	III(+)	ii°
		vii°

(2) Write two minor chord tables for the keys of B Minor and D Minor.

B minor

D minor

LESSON SIXTEEN

FIGURING

The procedure of indicating the inversion of any chord by noting the distances between the lowest note and the various notes placed above it, is known as FIGURING. Chord Figuring is a shorthand system that has been used since the 15th Century.

When you count the distances between the lowest note and the two notes placed above it in a three-note chord the following numbers appear:

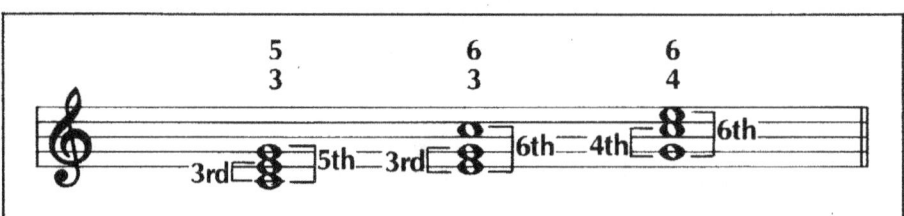

These numbers can then be placed alongside the degree number of the scale, so that the reader can instantly find out the type of chord, its position in the scale and its inversion.

For Example: I$^6_4$, would indicate a Major Chord on the First degree of a Major Scale, sounded in **Second Inversion.**

ii$^6_3$ would indicate a Minor Chord on the second degree, sounded in the **First Inversion**.

THE STANDARD SYSTEM FOR TRIADS
In most cases when sounding a triad, the Root Position Figuring is taken to be understood, while in the First Inversion the number 3 is also taken to be understood. Therefore when indicating the three positions of the chord you need only write the degree number for the Root Position Chord, and the degree number plus the number 6 for the First Inversion Chord. The full figuring and the degree number must appear, however for the Second Inversion Chord.

e.g. Root Position = **IV**;   1st Inversion = **IV**^{6};   Second Inversion = **IV**$^6_4$

THE SUSPENDED FOURTH TRIAD
As this triad is not composed of the same distances as the MAJOR, MINOR, DIMINISHED and AUGMENTED triads, it has to be figured a different way. Most often in Classical Music, simply the number 4 will appear to indicate that the Third degree in the triad is to be replaced by the Fourth.

FIGURING FOR SEVENTH CHORDS
The following diagram shows the Root Position and three inversions of the Seventh chord shape. The intervals from the lowest note to each note above it are given.

N.B. Arrow Marks the Root note.

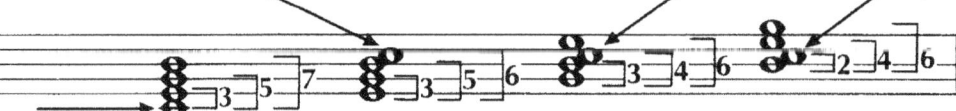

From these intervals, the 'figuring' for 7th chords is taken. Below are the 'figures' for the Root Position and inversions of the 7ths. The numbers which are understood are in brackets.

Root Pos.	1st Inv.	2nd Inv.	3rd Inv.
7	6	(6)	(6)
(5)	5	4	4
(3)	(3)	3	2

Thus the standard figuring for the above is:—

Root Pos.	1st Inv.	2nd Inv.	3rd Inv.
7	6	4	4
	5	3	2

LESSON SEVENTEEN

EXERCISES ON CHORD TABLES AND FIGURING

The following questions are divided into four sections:
1. Work out the key of each line of music. The Key Signature and Final chord will confirm the key.
2. Write the Chord Table for the key. Be careful to use the Major Table or the Minor Table in accordance with your finding for 1.
3. Name all the chords, placing the chord symbols above the chords as shown in the example.
4. Place the Degree number and Figuring in the area below each chord, also as shown in the example.

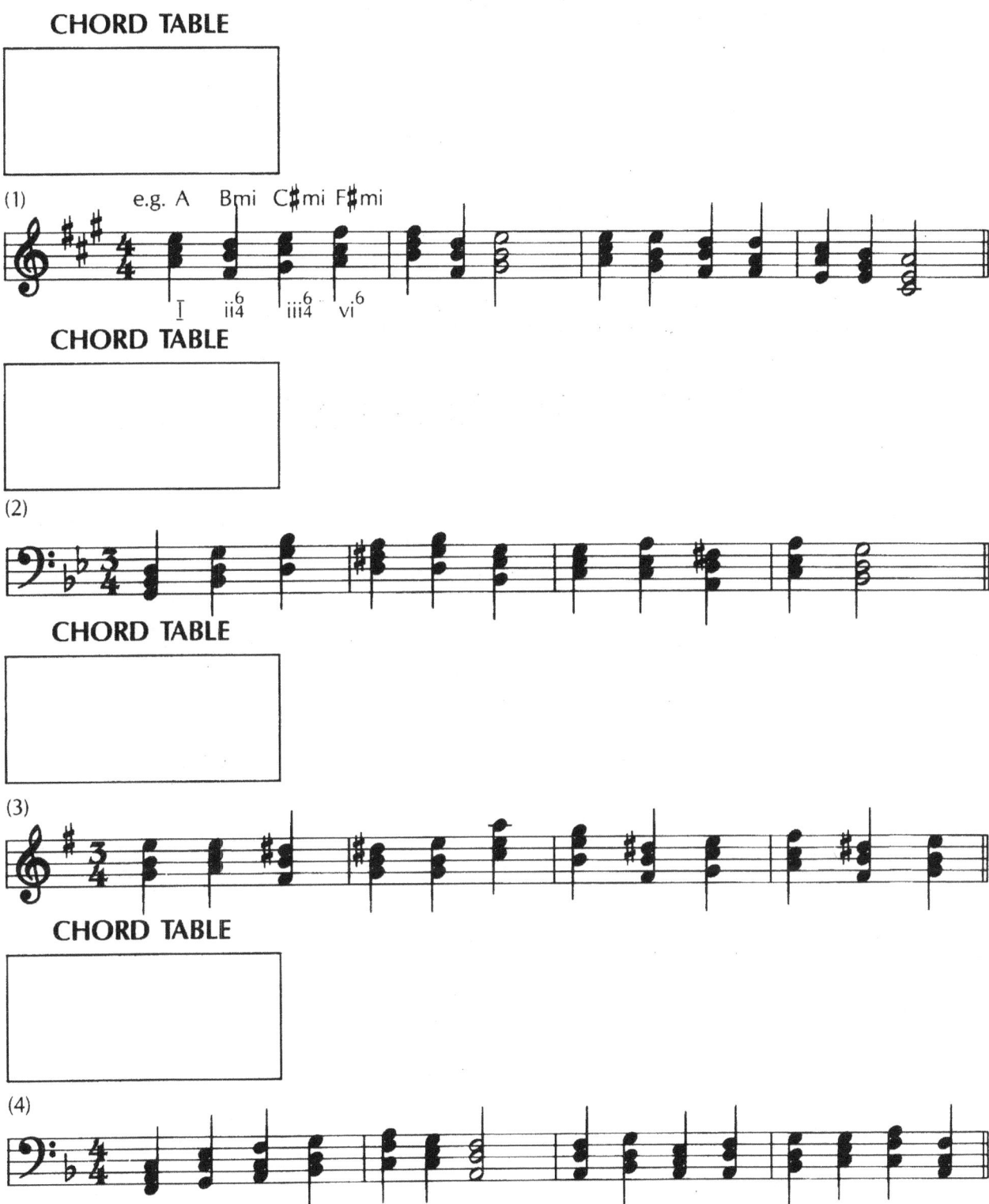

LESSON EIGHTEEN

THE TWO SMALLEST NOTE VALUES
64th Notes and Rests; 128th Notes and Rests

This chart shows the relative values of the smaller value notes compared to a Quarter Note or Crotchet. Multiply the number of notes on the chart by FOUR to arrive at the number of notes per WHOLE NOTE.

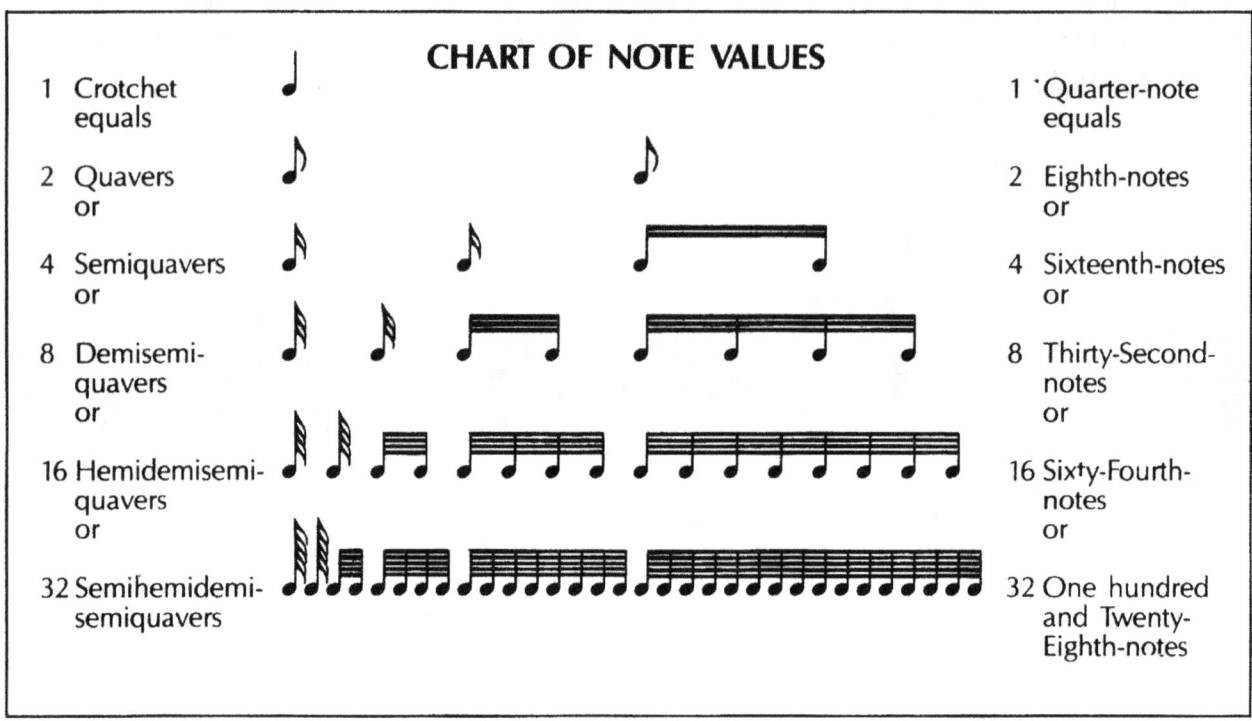

The 64th Note or Hemidemisemiquaver   (Note ; Rest)

After the 32nd note the next smallest size is the 64th note or Hemidemisemiquaver. Referring to the chart above you can see that 64 of them fit into the time taken by a Whole Note.

The Note has FOUR tails and the rest has FOUR hooks.

The 128th Note or Semihemidemisemiquaver   (Note ; Rest)

The very smallest note value that is ever used is the 128th note or Semihemidemisemiquaver. (At this point in time it makes far more sense to use the American System of time names, i.e. 128th note). 128 of them fit into the time taken by a Whole Note.

The Note has FIVE tails and the rest has FIVE hooks.

EXERCISE

Identify these notes and rests.

(1) = ...   (2) = ...

(2) = ...   (4) = ...

(5) = ...   (6) = ...

(7) = ...   (8) = ...

LESSON NINETEEN

RARER NOTES AND RESTS

The Breve or Double Whole Note   (Note 𝄺 ; Rest ▬)

In Book One of this series I mentioned the Breve in the discussion on 4/2 time. You would be likely to encounter a Breve in music of the time of J.S. Bach or earlier; that is before 1750.

The Breve is double the length of a Semibreve and therefore would receive 8 crotchet or quarter note counts. It would occupy a whole bar in 4/2 time, (four minims or half notes).

It is interesting to note that the word Breve comes from the French word 'Bref' meaning short and that there were larger note values (for instance the 'Long' ▌) in use in earlier times. More information on this topic is available in the Oxford Companion to Music. Edited by Percy Scholes.

The Alternative Quarter Rest or Crotchet Rest

In some older publications you will see the Crotchet Rest written like this ╿ The rest looks like a reversed Quaver or Eighth Note Rest.

◆◆◆◆◆◆◆◆◆◆◆◆◆◆◆◆◆◆◆◆◆◆

EXERCISES

(1) Name these notes and rests.

1. 𝄺 = ...   2. ╿ = ...   3. ▬ ....

(2) Write the following notes and rests.

   (a) 32nd rest .... (b) breve .... (c) 128th note ....

   (d) two types of crotchet rest .... , ... (e) 64th note ....

(3) Referring to the chart of Relative Note values on the previous page, figure out the answers to the following questions.

   (a) How many 64th notes take up the time of one Eighth Note? ....

   (b) How many 128th notes take up the time of one Quarter Note? ....

   (c) How many 32nd notes take up the time of one Eighth Note? ....

   (d) How many 128th notes take up the time of one Sixteenth Note? ....

   (e) How many 128th notes take up the time of one Eighth Note? ....

LESSON TWENTY

THE PENTATONIC SCALE

The Pentatonic Scale is a five-note scale which is formed when five notes each the interval of a Perfect Fifth away from the next, are arranged as a scale. 'Penta' means 'five' and 'ton' means 'sound'.

For example, these notes which are a fifth apart, C G D A E can be arranged to form the Pentatonic Scale on C: C D E G A.

If the Scale is begun on F♯, the resulting notes, F♯ G♯ A♯ C♯ D♯ happen to be all the black notes within one octave on a keyboard.

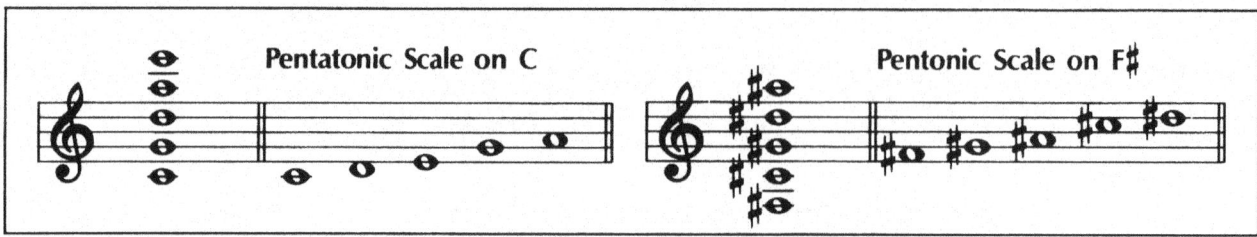

The scale is a very pleasant sounding scale, which contains no elements of tension. Comparing the Pentatonic Scale on C to the Major Scale on C, you find that the 4th and 7th notes of the Major Scale are the ones that are omitted.

It is the 4th and 7th degrees of the Major Scale which together form the interval of a TRITONE (Aug 4, or Dim 5). The Tritone has a very strong leading function which requires almost immediate resolution. Therefore, if the Tritone is avoided in a scale such as the Pentatonic Scale, pleasant melodies which tend to 'float' and can be extended for quite some time without the need for definite punctuation marks such as Cadences. Much of the music of Japan, China, Indonesia and other countries in the region makes use of the Pentatonic Scale.

The scale is also very popular in the FOLK MUSIC of such countries as England, Scotland, Ireland and America.

Here is a short list of tunes for you to find, which make use of the Pentatonic Scale. Ye Banks and Ye Braes (Scottish), My Bonnie Coukoo (Irish), Auld Land Syne (Scottish), Git Along, Little Dogies and The Lone Star Trail (both Traditional Cowboy Songs) and Swing Low, Sweet Chariot, Deep River and Little David (all Negro Spirituals).

◆◆◆◆◆◆◆◆◆◆◆◆◆◆◆◆◆◆◆◆◆◆◆◆◆◆◆◆

EXERCISES

First write the Major Scale beginning on the given starting notes, then form the Pentatonic Scales on the same starting notes by omitting the 4th and 7th degrees.

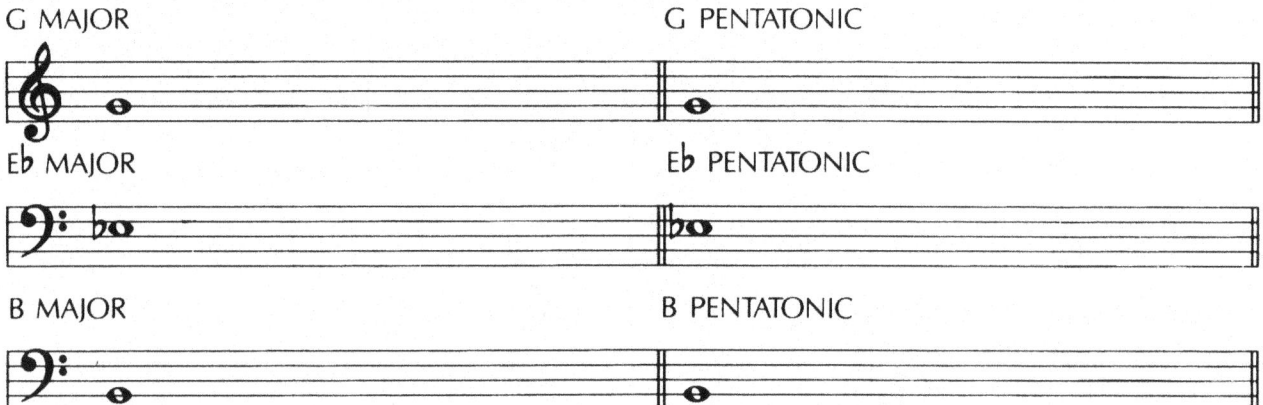

THE BLUES SCALE

The Blues Scale is one which incorporates the Flattened or 'Blue' notes of African Scales. In the African Scales the Flattened Notes are sung anywhere between the Flattened Version of the note and the Major Scale degree; for instance a quarter tone away from the traditionally notated sound.

The Scale is notated sometimes with a Sharpened Fourth degree and sometimes with a Flattened Fifth Degree. Some versions of the scale include the second degree of the scale as well. I have written the second degree in brackets bacause of the fact that it is not always used.

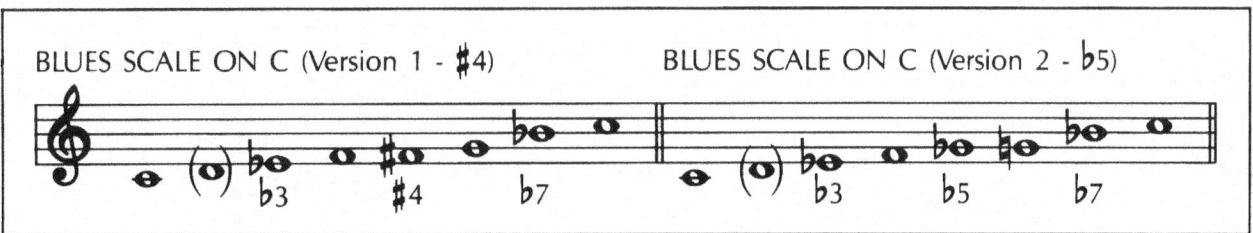

Notice also that the sixth degree of the Major Scale is omitted.

The Blues Scale is usually played over the Primary Triads in a Major Key, so that there are several 'clashes' of sound when the Flattened 3rd, Flattened 5th and Flattened 7th degrees are sounded against the unflattened notes in the corresponding chord. This explains also why when playing a Blues Progression using the Primary Chords of the Key, each chord is often played as a Dominant Seventh; in other words the Major Triad plus the Flattened Seventh degree from the Blues Scale.

EXERCISES

Write both the Major Scale and the Blues Scale beginning on the given starting notes. Use the Version required; i.e. Version 1 or 2.

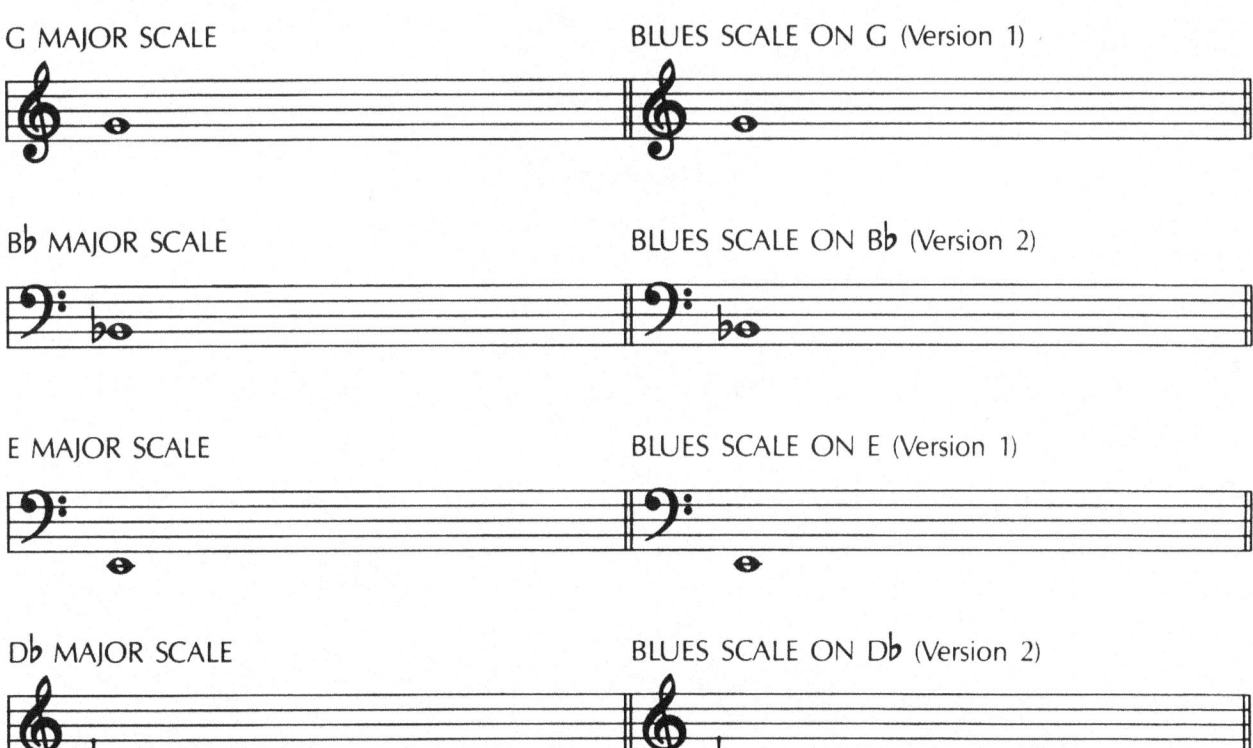

LESSON TWENTY-TWO

SWING TIMING

Much popular music in the first half of the 20th Century and on into the present day is written and played with a 'Swing' feel. That is, music is interpreted with a bounce which can be written as a Triplet figure.

The types of music included here are Boogie-Woogie, Blues, Shuffle and Swing Jazz. Depending on the musical figure required the composer may choose to use:

a straight quaver (8th) notation:

or the dotted quaver followed by a semiquaver:

or the strictly correct (in the classical sense) uneven triplet notation:

If the music is marked 'Swing', all of these rhythms will be counted the same way with a Triplet feel. That is, in 4/4 1+a 2+a 3+a 4+a.

e.g. 		
1+a 2+a 3+a 4+a	1+a 2+a 3+a 4+a	1+a 2+a 3+a 4+a
Here the first quaver is given 2/3rds of the triplet and the second quaver the remaining 1/3rd.	Here the dotted quaver is given 2/3rds and the semiquaver the remaining 1/3rd.	This is played as written.

*N.B. If 16ths occur in this figure ♩♫ they are played on the last third of the triplet ♩♫
                                                                                         1 + a

If they occur in this figure in Swing Timing ♫♩

they are played on the first third of the triplet thus: ♫♩
                                                         1 + a

◆◆◆◆◆◆◆◆◆◆◆◆◆◆◆◆◆◆◆◆◆◆◆◆◆◆◆◆◆◆◆

EXERCISE

Continue the counting under these bars of music which are to be played in Swing Timing, then clap or play the rhythms through.

LESSON TWENTY-THREE

THE WHOLE-TONE SCALE

This scale, as the name suggests is made up entirely of Whole-Tones between each degree of the scale. The scale contains only six notes owing to the fact that there are only twelve semitones in an Octave and therefore 'six' tones.

There are only two basic forms of the scale. One beginning on C and another beginning on D♭. Below are the two scales and their keyboard patterns.

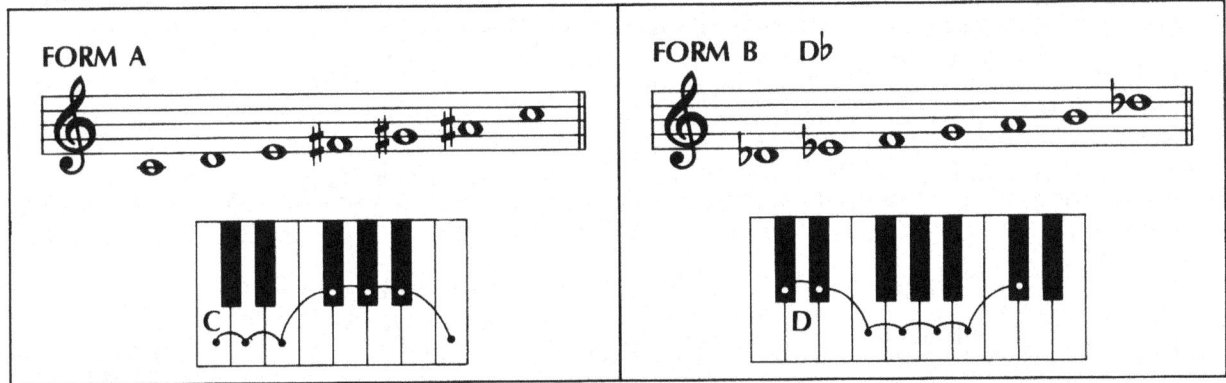

If each scale is begun on another starting note the notation may alter but the keyboard pattern remains the same.

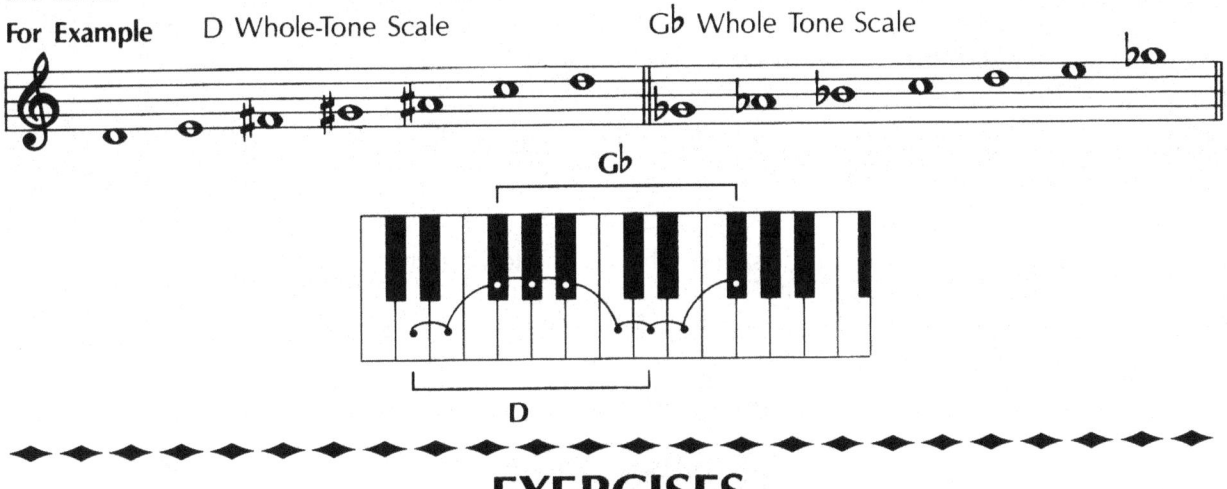

EXERCISES

Write Whole-Tone Scales beginning on the given starting notes. Indicate whether the written scale belongs to either Form A or Form B.

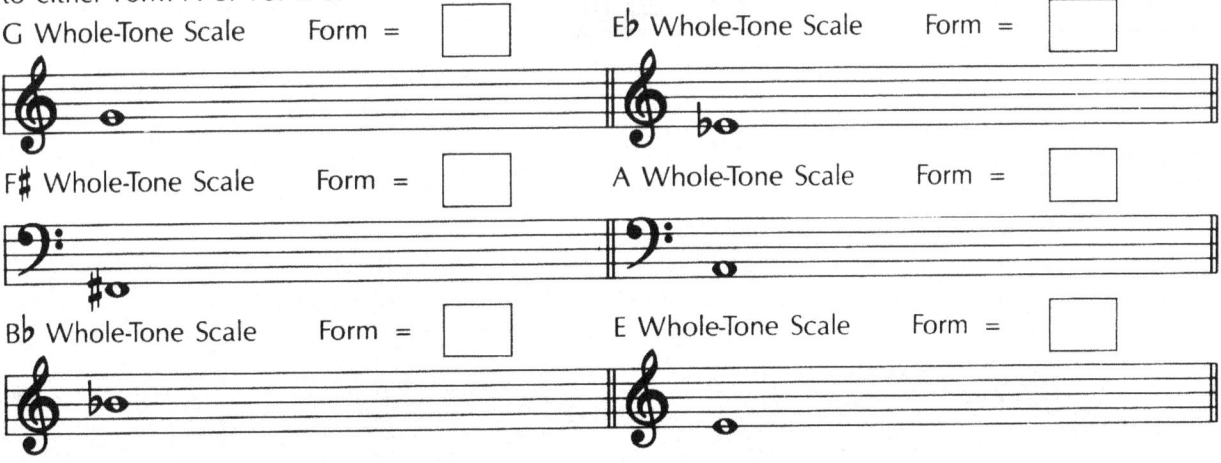

LESSON TWENTY-FOUR

THE DIMINISHED SCALE

The Diminished Scale is another scale in which the Tones and Semitones fall in a regular pattern. It has been used by several Twentieth Century Composers, the most notable of which is the French composer Olivier Messian who regarded this scale as a 'Mode of Limited Transposition'. (The Whole-Tone Scale is also a Mode of Limited Transposition.)

This term is explained when you notice that the Basic Form of the Scale has the pattern T S T S T S T S and that by playing this pattern on any three neighbouring Semitones or any three neighbouring keys in the Cycle of Fifths, all the forms of the scale are covered.

The only variation of the pattern that occurs is that it can be commenced with the Semitone so that the scale moves S T S T S T S T.

An easy way to remember the scale pattern in it's basic form is to think of the scale as using the first four notes of two minor scales each the interval of a Diminished 5th or Augmented 4th (TRITONE) away from each other.

For instance the first four notes of C Minor Scale and the first four notes of F♯ Minor Scale.

C DIMINISHED SCALE (Basic Form Whole-Step, Half-Step)

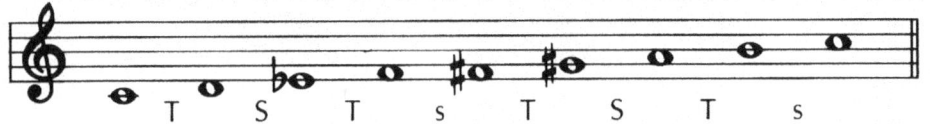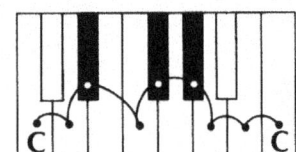

C DIMINISHED SCALE (Alternate Form Half-Step, Whole-Step)

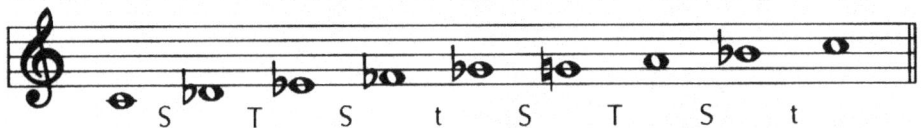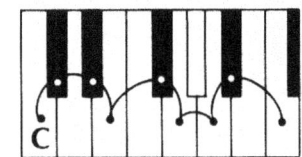

The Scale is widely used in Jazz Improvisation when the following chord types appear; Basic Form — Dim7 and Half Dim7 (mi7♭5), Dim9, mi9♭5. Alternative Form — Dom7♯9 and Dom7♭9 chords. (See Book 2 of Contemporary Chord Workbook series by Margaret Brandman, for more information on Extended Chords such as Ninths.)

◆◆◆◆◆◆◆◆◆◆◆◆◆◆◆◆◆◆◆◆◆◆◆◆◆◆◆◆

EXERCISES

(1) Write the Basic Form of the Diminished Scale beginning on A, E and B.

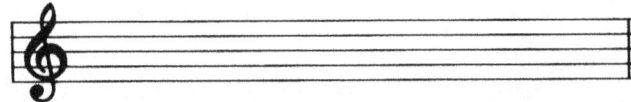

(2) Identify these scales as either the Basic Form or the Alternate Form of the Diminished Scale.

(a) .... (b) .... (c) ....

LESSON TWENTY-FIVE

COMPARING THE SIMPLE AND COMPOUND TIME SIGNATURES
6/4 AND 3/2; 6/8 AND 3/4

When writing out music or transcribing music from a record or tape, one often has to decide whether music contains SIX PULSES to the bar is in SIMPLE TRIPLE time or COMPOUND DUPLE time.

If you refer to Lessons 15 and 16 in Book 3 of this series, you will recall the discussion on this topic.

The basic feature which differentiates a Simple Triple Time-Signature from a Compound Duple Time-Signature, is the grouping of the pulses into groups of TWO (Simple Time) or THREE (Compound Time).

If you are presented with a question which requires you to write the timing under the notes and supply the Time-Signature, I suggest you always try counting the bar as a COMPOUND DUPLE Time-Signature **first.** Then if the counts do **not** fall into the pattern 1 2 3 (Imaginary Bar Line) 4 5 6, rework the exercise counting 1 & 2 & 3 & .

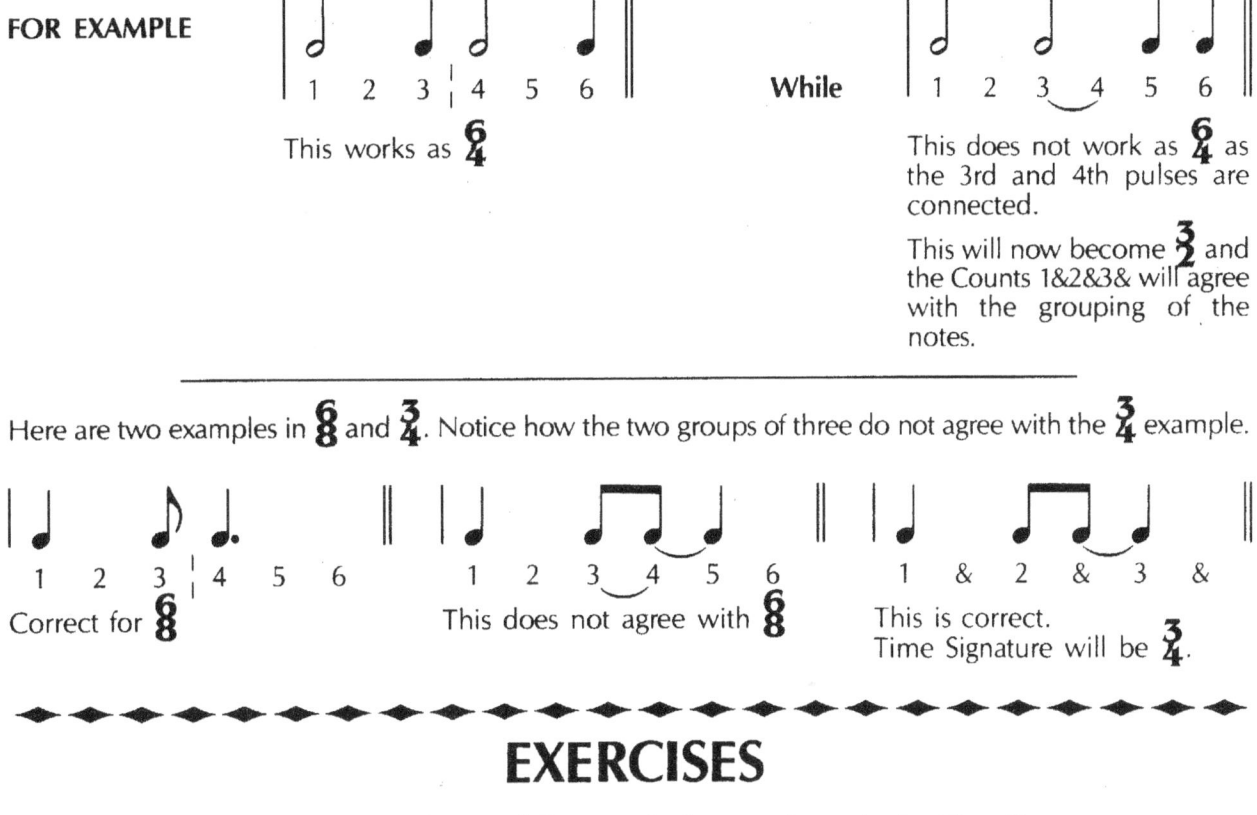

Here are two examples in 6/8 and 3/4. Notice how the two groups of three do not agree with the 3/4 example.

EXERCISES

Write the Timing under the bars for the following rhythms and supply the Time-Signatures.

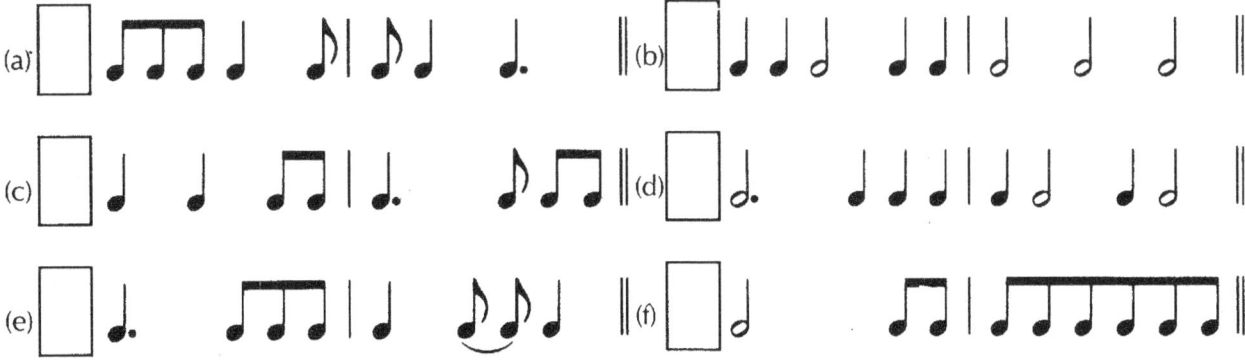

LESSON TWENTY-SIX

NAMING INTERVALS WITHIN A LINE OF MUSIC

When naming intervals in a line of music one must keep in mind that the Key Signature of the piece is only relevant to the extent that it makes you aware of the notes being used in the piece. The intervals will not necessarily relate to that Key Signature directly.

EACH INTERVAL MUST BE TAKEN AS A SEPARATE ENTITY AND BE WORKED OUT FROM THE LOWER OF THE TWO NOTES WHICH COMPRISE THE INTERVAL.

As we saw in Part A of this Book the terms Major and Minor when applied to intervals mean 'Greater' and 'Lesser'. We also saw that Minor Intervals do not necessarily belong to a Minor Scale.

Here is a line of music with each interval named according to Quantity (size) and Quality.

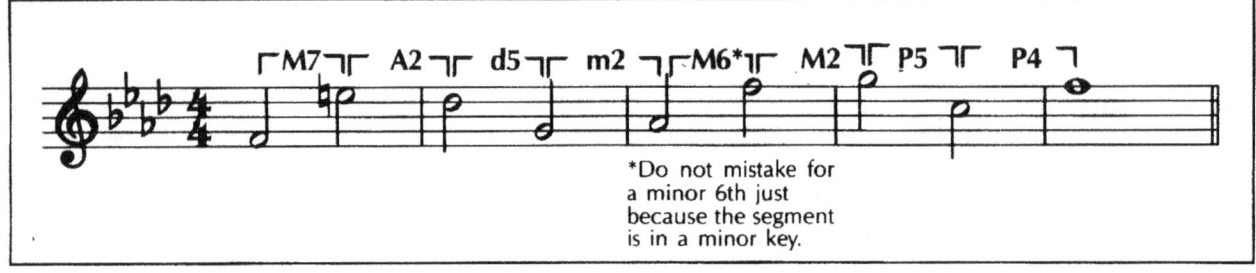

*Do not mistake for a minor 6th just because the segment is in a minor key.

EXERCISES

Name the bracketted intervals giving Quality and Quantity, in the following lines of music.

(1)

(2)
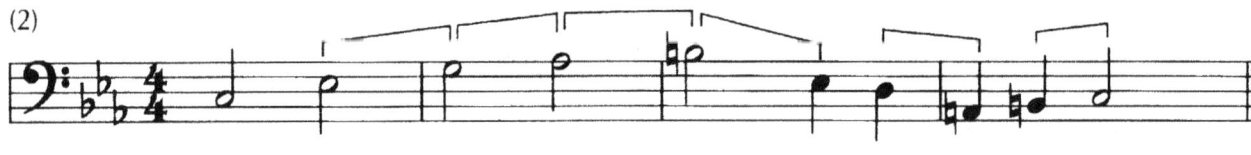

(3)

LESSON TWENTY-SEVEN
INVERSIONS OF COMPOUND INTERVALS

In Lesson Two in Part A of this book, the topic of Compound Intervals was introduced. As you will recall a Compound Interval is one with a numerical value **larger than** an Octave.

Here are the Compound Intervals from the Ninth to the Fifteenth taken from the Major Scale.

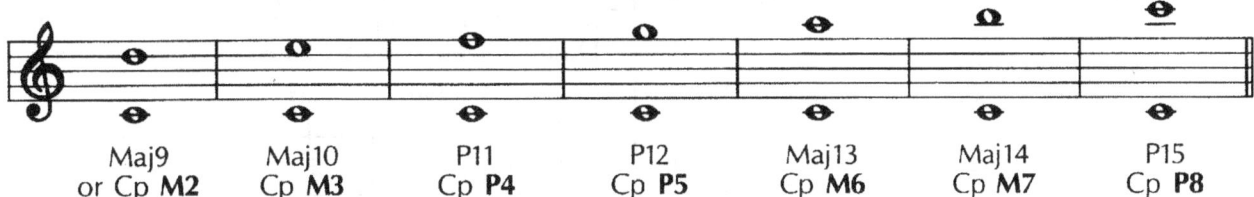

INVERSIONS OF COMPOUND INTERVALS
To invert a Compound Interval, take the lower note UP **two octaves** or the upper note DOWN **two octaves.**

For Example: - A Major 10th or Cp M3 becomes a Minor 6th. The same way as a Simple M3 becomes m6.
           - A P11 or Cp P4 becomes P5.
           - An Aug12th or Cp Aug5 becomes a dim4.

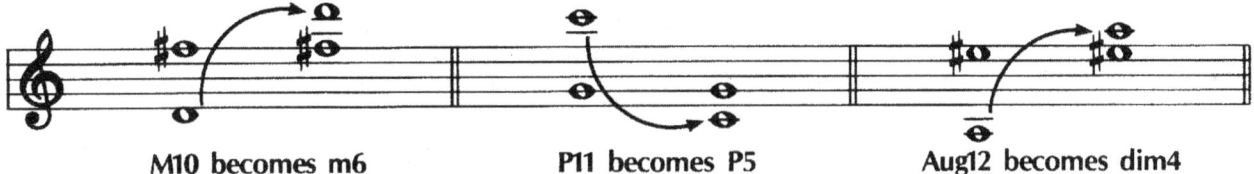

All the features which occur when inverting a Simple Interval occur in the same way when inverting Compound Intervals. Check with Lesson 27 in Book 3 of this series.

◆◆◆◆◆◆◆◆◆◆◆◆◆◆◆◆◆◆◆◆◆◆

EXERCISES

(1) Name these Compound Intervals.

(2) Name these Compound Intervals, then invert them and name their inversions.

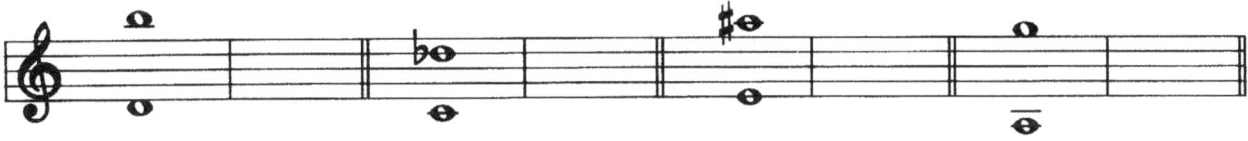

(3) Complete these sentences.

    When inverted a: - Cp M2 (M9) becomes a ....

                      - Cp m3 (m10) becomes a ....

                      - Cp d4 (d11) becomes an ....

                      - Cp P5 (P12) becomes a ....

                      - Cp m6 (m13) becomes a ....

                      - Cp M7 (M14) becomes a ....

                      - Cp P8 (P15) becomes a ....

LESSON TWENTY-EIGHT

INTRODUCTION TO HARMONY — PERFECT AND PLAGAL CADENCES

Many pieces of music are based upon the three Primary Chords of the key. Refer to Lesson 12 to 15 in Part B of this book for the information on the Primary Chords and the Chord Tables for Major and Minor keys.

In a Major Key a simple four-bar tune may use a progression such as the following.

In a Minor Key the same progression would use minor chords on degrees i and iv and the Dominant chord would still be a Major Chord.

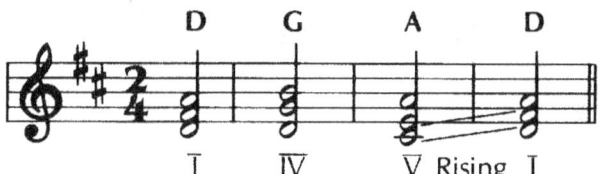
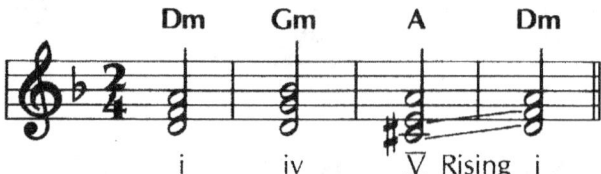

In these examples the final two chords are chords V and I (i). When used in this way at the end of a tune, the two chords form a CADENCE or Ending Formula. The specific cadence which moves from V to I (i) is called a PERFECT CADENCE. It has a rising feeling and as it can be used at the very end of a piece of music it is known as Full Close.

If the Chord Progression moved in this manner I V IV I (Major Keys) or i V iv i (minor Keys), the final two chords would form another type of Cadence known as a PLAGAL CADENCE. This Cadence is also remembered as the AMEN Cadence as the two chords used on the words AMEN in most hymn tunes are chords IV and I. This type of Cadence has a falling feeling.

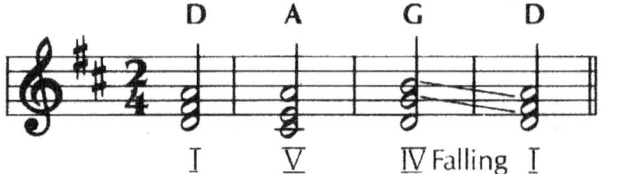
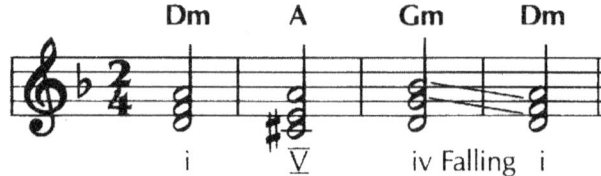

To play the above examples in PIANO STYLE, simply add the Root Note of each chord in the Bass Clef.

◆◆◆◆◆◆◆◆◆◆◆◆◆◆◆◆◆◆◆◆◆◆◆◆◆◆◆◆◆◆◆

EXERCISES

(1) Give the degree numbers of the two chords which form:

   (a) A Perfect Cadence — .... (Major Key); .... (Minor Key)

   (b) A Plagal Cadence — .... (Major Key); .... (Minor Key)

(2) (a) Write the Primary Chords in the sequence found in the Chord Table for the key of this piece.
    (b) Write the degree numbers **under** each chord and the chord names **above** each chord in the piece.
    (c) Name the Cadence used. ANSWER ....

CHORD TABLE

(3) Follow the same procedure as for the previous question. Name the Cadence ....

CHORD TABLE

LESSON TWENTY-NINE

THE USE OF SECONDARY CHORDS AND THE IMPERFECT CADENCE

Longer pieces of music often make use of the secondary chords, as found on the lower rows of the Chord Table, for interest, variety and Aural colour. Many tunes have Chord Progressions based upon the Cycle of Fifths. A frequent progression is one that moves vi - ii - V̲ - I̲ (Major Keys) or V̲I̲ - ii⁰ - V̲ - i (Minor Keys).

For instance in C Major: (C) Am Dmi G   C
                         (I) vi ii   V̲   I̲

THE IMPERFECT CADENCE — Half Close

In order to sustain interest in a longer piece of music, most pieces make use of an intermediary Cadence that has the feeling of ending a section, but not finalising the piece. A set of chord progressions which fall into this category are all known as IMPERFECT CADENCES.

The main feature of an Imperfect Cadence is that it ends on the Dominant (V̲) chord. The following are Imperfect Cadences: I̲ - V̲; ii - V̲; I̲V̲ - V̲; vi - V̲ (Major Keys) and i - V̲; ii⁰ - V̲; iv - V̲; and V̲I̲ - V̲ (Minor Keys).

Here is an example of an eight bar tune which uses an Imperfect Cadence in the **middle** and a Perfect Cadence at the **end**.

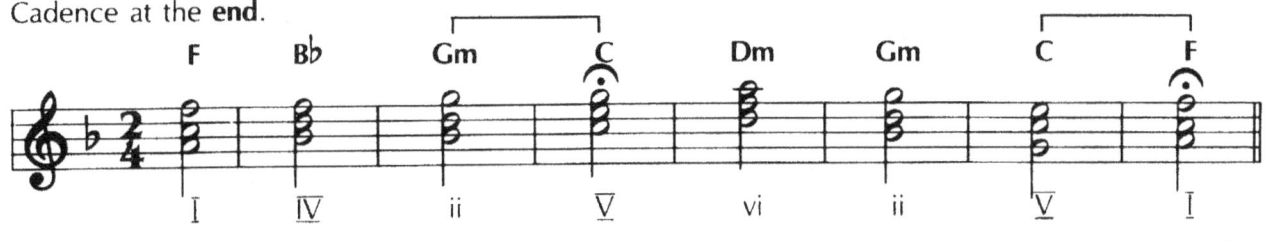

◆◆◆◆◆◆◆◆◆◆◆◆◆◆◆◆◆◆◆◆◆◆◆◆◆◆◆◆◆◆◆

EXERCISES

(1) Name the following Cadences as either Perfect, Plagal or Imperfect. Also indicate whether they belong to Major Keys or Minor Keys. Refer once again to the Chord Tables for both Major and Minor Keys to help you work out the question.

e.g. ii - V̲ = Imp - Major Key

I̲V̲ - I̲ = ...   i - V̲   = ...
V̲ - i   = ...   V̲I̲ - V̲ = ...
I̲V̲ - V̲ = ...   ii⁰ - V̲ = ...
I̲ - V̲   = ...   iv - i = ...

(2) (a) Write the full Chord Table for this piece in a Major Key.
    (b) Write the degree numbers **under** each chord and the chord names **above** each chord in the piece.
    (c) Name the two cadences used. (1) .... (2) ....

CHORD TABLE

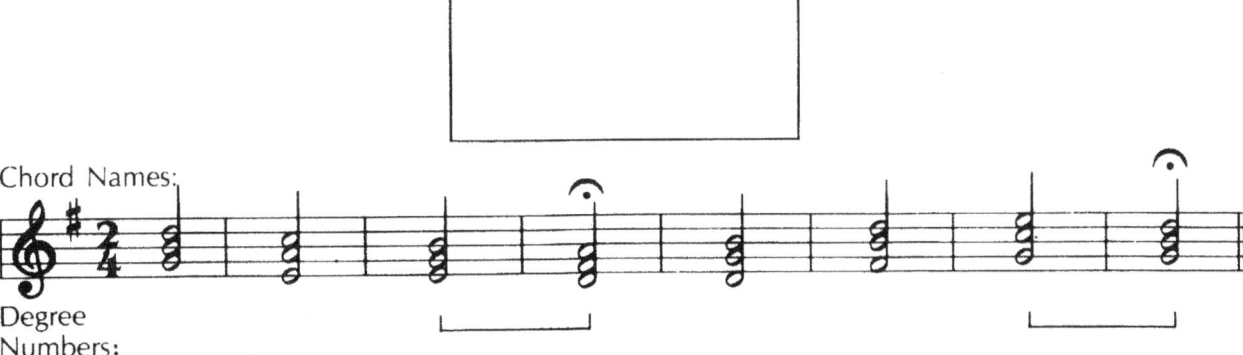

Chord Names:

Degree Numbers:

LESSON THIRTY

THE INTERRUPTED OR SURPRISE CADENCE

There is another type of intermediary Cadence that is used to bring sections within the body of the music to a close. The Cadence is known by several names including INTERRUPTED, SURPRISE AND DECEPTIVE.

The chord progression for the Cadence is from V to vi (Major Keys) and from V to VI (Minor Keys). The use of Chord V tends to *deceive* the listener into believing that a Perfect Cadence will follow, while the effect of the movement to chord vi gives the listener a *surprise* and the music then feels as if it has been *interrupted*.

The Cadence is often used to end the **first** quarter of a piece of music, or to end the **third** quarter. For instance in a Sixteen Bar tune it would be likely to occur at either the fourth or twelfth bars.

Here is an example of a sixteen bar tune which uses Interrupted, Imperfect and Plagal Cadences.

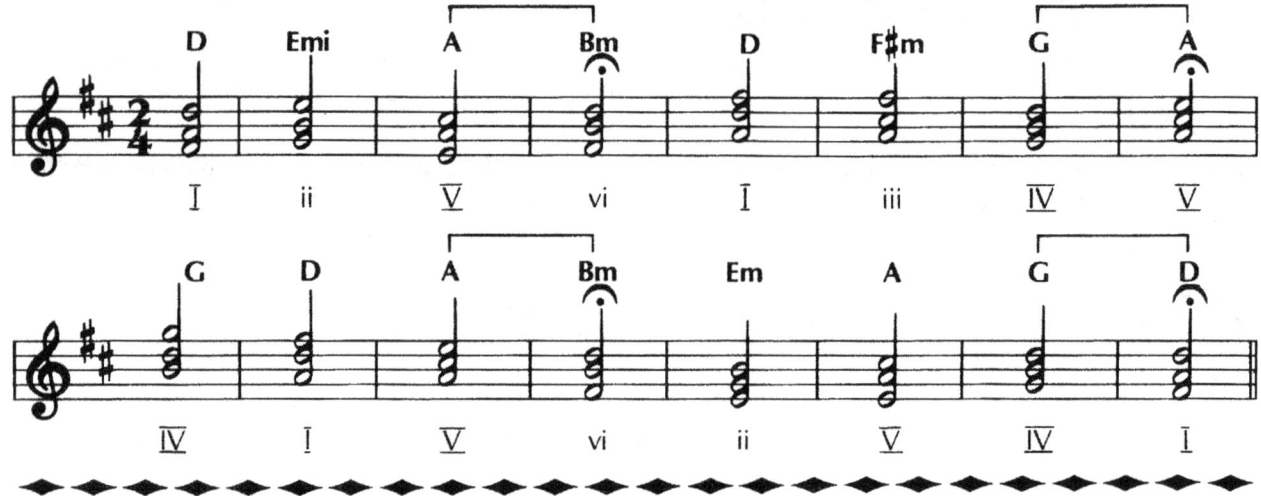

EXERCISES

(1) Give the degree numbers of the Interrupted Cadence in a

   Major Key .... Is chord **six** a Major or Minor Chord? ....

(2) Give the degree numbers of the Interrupted Cadence in a

   Minor Key .... Is chord **six** a Major or Minor Chord? ....

(3) Indicate the types of Cadences and whether they belong to Major or Minor Keys.

   V - VI   = ...   ii - V   = ...

   iv - i   = ...   V - vi   = ...

   V - I   = ...   i - V   = ...

(4) Complete these chord progressions by writing in the notes of the required chords. Indicate the key of each progression in the space provided and place the chords names above the bars.

LESSON THIRTY-ONE
EXERCISES ON CHORD PROGRESSIONS AND CADENCES

(1) (a) Write the full Chord Table for this piece in a Minor Key.
   (b) Write the degree numbers **under** each chord and the chord names **above** each chord in the piece.
   (c) Name the four cadences used.

   (1) .... (2) .... (3) .... (4) ....

CHORD TABLE

(2) (a) Write the full Chord Table for this piece in a Major Key.
   (b) Write the degree numbers **under** each chord and the chord names **above** as was done in the previous exercise.
   (c) Name the four cadences used.

   (1) .... (2) .... (3) .... (4) ....

CHORD TABLE

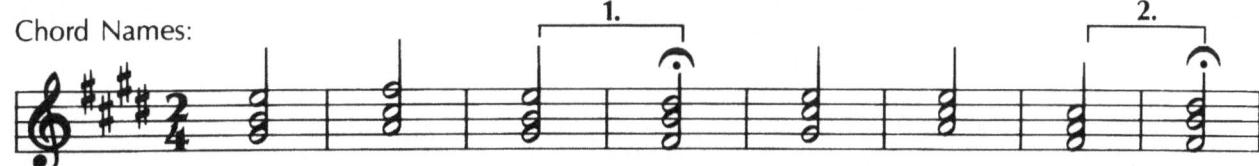

'HARMONY COMES TOGETHER' Students who have completed this page will have gained sufficient music theory foundations to begin learning to write four-part harmony. Margaret Brandman's book *Harmony Comes Together* (MMP 8081) provides instruction in the topic of four-part harmony approached from the point of view of Root Progressions brought to life with a unique colour coding system. *Harmony Comes Together* includes plenty of exercises to allow the student to become proficient in writing chord progressions and cadences arranged for four voices.

LESSON THIRTY-TWO
ACOUSTICS

Listed below are some of the basic terms associated with Acoustics, along with brief definitions of their meanings.

ACOUSTICS — the science of sound.

VIBRATION — a to and fro quivering. If an object strikes another object, vibrations occur. These are then transferred to the air in waves. If the sound is loud enough, the vibrations travel to our ears and cause our ear drums to vibrate, giving the sensation of **sound**.
— regular vibrations produce musical sounds, while irregular vibrations produce what we perceive as noise.

FREQUENCY — how fast or often the vibrations are travelling. (The speed).
— faster vibrations = higher sounds.
— slower vibrations = lower sounds.

AMPLITUDE — the size of the vibrations.
— larger back and forth movements = louder sound.
— smaller back and forth movements = softer sound.

Here is a diagram of a wave showing the Frequency and the Amplitude.

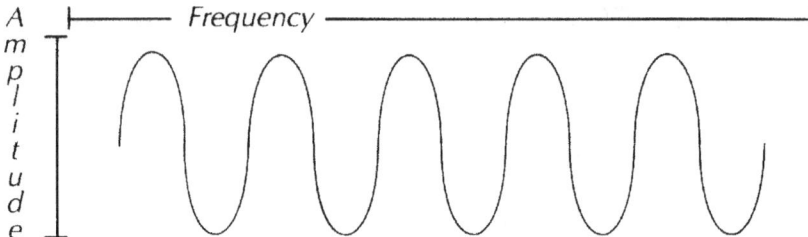

TIMBRE — tone colour or texture of sound. This is affected by the types of harmonics present in addition to the fundamental note.

Refer to Book 2 of my CONTEMPORARY CHORD WORKBOOK series for more information on the Harmonic Series and Timbre.

PARTS OF A MUSICAL INSTRUMENT
(1) One or more *Vibrators* (source of sound)
(2) A *Resonator* which amplifies the sound.
(3) The human voice also has an *Articulator* or means of forming words.
Applied to two instruments: the Vibrators in a Piano are the strings and the Resonator is the Wooden outer shell of the piano. In a Clarinet the Vibrator is the Reed in the Mouthpiece and the Resonator is the body of the instrument.

EXERCISES

Complete these sentences.

(1) The **size** of the vibrations is known as the ....

(2) The **speed** of the vibrations is the ....

(3) Timbre means ....

(4) The science of sound is known as ....

(5) A .... is a 'to and fro quivering'.

(6) The vibrators on a Violin are the ....

(7) The body of the Violin forms the ....

(8) In a human voice the means of forming the words is known as the ....

LESSON THIRTY-THREE

ORNAMENTS

These two pages briefly list the main Ornaments found in the music of the Baroque and Classical periods. (1650-1820 approx.)

In the keyboard music of the period which was written for clavichord, harpsichord and the very early pianos, the problems of lack of sustain and inability to obtain sudden emphasis were overcome by the use of these ornaments. For instance a Trill would give the impression that a note was being sustained as the main note was repeated several times in alternation with the secondary note.

Acciaccatura (It. "to crush")

The small note with the line through its stem. Also known as a GRACE Note or CRUSHED Note. Played with the smaller note 'crushed' onto the following note. Still used today to emphasise a principal note.

Appoggiatura (It. "to lean on")

The smaller note takes a minimum of one-half the value of the principal note. If the principal note is dotted the Appoggiatura takes two-thirds of the value. It is played **on** the beat.

Trill (**tr** or **tr**~~~~)

The principal note and the note above are played in alternating fashion for the duration of the written note. In music prior to 1750 the Trill was begun on the upper note, while in later music it generally begins on the lower.

Mordent (Upper Mordent or Schneller)

The principal note is alternated rapidly with the scale step above.

The original meaning of this ornament was that it signified a Trill. (17th Century). However it has since been taken to mean an Upper Mordent.

Inverted Mordent

The principal note is alternated rapidly with the scale step below.

Accidentals If notes other than scale tone notes are to be used in an ornament, the required accidental is written **above** the ornament if it refers to the note above the principal note, and **below** the ornament if it refers to the note below.

For Example — = play the sharpened version of the upper note.

EXERCISE

Match these ornaments to their correct names.

1. = ... (a) Acciaccatura (Crushed Note)
2. = ... (b) Lower Mordent
3. = ... (c) Appoggiatura
4. = ... (d) Trill
5. = ... (e) Mordent

LESSON THIRTY-FOUR
MORE ORNAMENTS

Turn (Grupetto) ∽

The usual manner in which a Turn is played, is to take the principal note the note above, the principal note again, the note below and finishing once again on the principal note. These notes are all played in the time of the written note. Some turns begin on the upper note and only contain four notes.

There are several rhythmic variations in the execution of the turn. Most editions give the suggested version required for each specific piece.

Inverted Turn ⇗ or ⇙

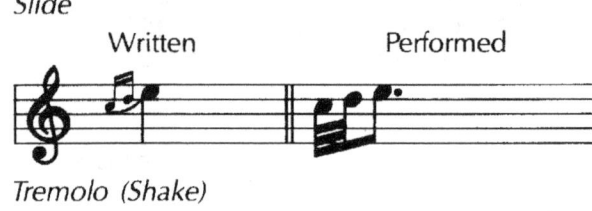

In an inverted turn the order of notes is reversed. P (Principal) Lower Note, P, Upper Note, P.

Slide

The Slide consists of two or more grace notes placed before the principal note. They are played on the beat, taking their time value from the principal note.

Tremolo (Shake)

A Tremolo is similar to a Trill, the only difference being that the two (or more notes involved are more than a Second apart. The sign is taken from the sign that string players use for a rapid bowing effect. This sign is still in use today.

SPECIAL NOTE ON ORNAMENTS

Most of the ornaments listed above are not found as a rule in music after the Classical Period, as these musical figures in the following periods, were written out in full and absorbed into general music notation.

◆◆◆◆◆◆◆◆◆◆◆◆◆◆◆◆◆◆◆◆◆◆

EXERCISE

Name these ornaments.

(1) = ...

(2) = ...

(3) = ...

(4) = ...

(5) = ...

(6) = ...

LESSON THIRTY-FIVE
TEST YOUR KNOWLEDGE

Answer the question or complete the sentence, whichever applies.

(1) The Minor Sounding Modes are .... , ... & ....

(2) Which two types of Cadences may be used at the very end of a piece of music? .... , ...

(3) Using Upper or Lower Case Roman Numerals as needed, give the degree numbers of the chords in the Upper Row of a Minor Chord Table ....

(4) Name the inversion of the interval of a Major 13th ....

(5) What notes are used in the Whole-Tone Scale beginning on D♭? ....

(6) What note or notes need to be altered to convert a Major Scale into a Lydian Mode? ....

(7) What are the degree numbers which comprise the four types of Imperfect Cadence in a Major Key? .... , ... , ... , ...

(8) What type of note is this ‖o‖? ....

(9) This ornament ( ) is known as .... or, ... or ....

(10) Which chord degree numbers are placed on the second horizontal row in a Major Chord Table? ....

(11) $^6_4$ represents a Triad in .... Inversion.

(12) Draw a 64th note. ....

(13) From which Mode is the Half-Diminished 7th (m7♭5) chord derived? ....

(14) Name this scale. ....

(15) Circle the syncopated areas in these bars of music.

(16) How many notes in a Pentatonic Scale? ....

(17) Which scale was regarded as a 'Mode of Limited Transposition' by Contemporary French composer Olivier Messian? ....

(18) In a double dotted note, what proportion of the value of the original note is the **second** dot worth? ....

(19) Supply the counts for this music in 4/4 that is to be played with a 'Swing Feel'.

(20) Give the figuring for a seventh chord in third inversion. ....

(21) Which type of triad is found as chord 'seven' in both Major and Minor Keys? ....

(22) How many hooks does a 128th rest have? ....

(23) Provide the Time Signature and the counts for these bars of music.

(24) By what three names is the Cadence which uses chords V to vi (Major Key) known? .... , ... and ....

(25) This ornament ( ) is known as ....

(26) The science of sound is known as ....

ANSWER SHEET

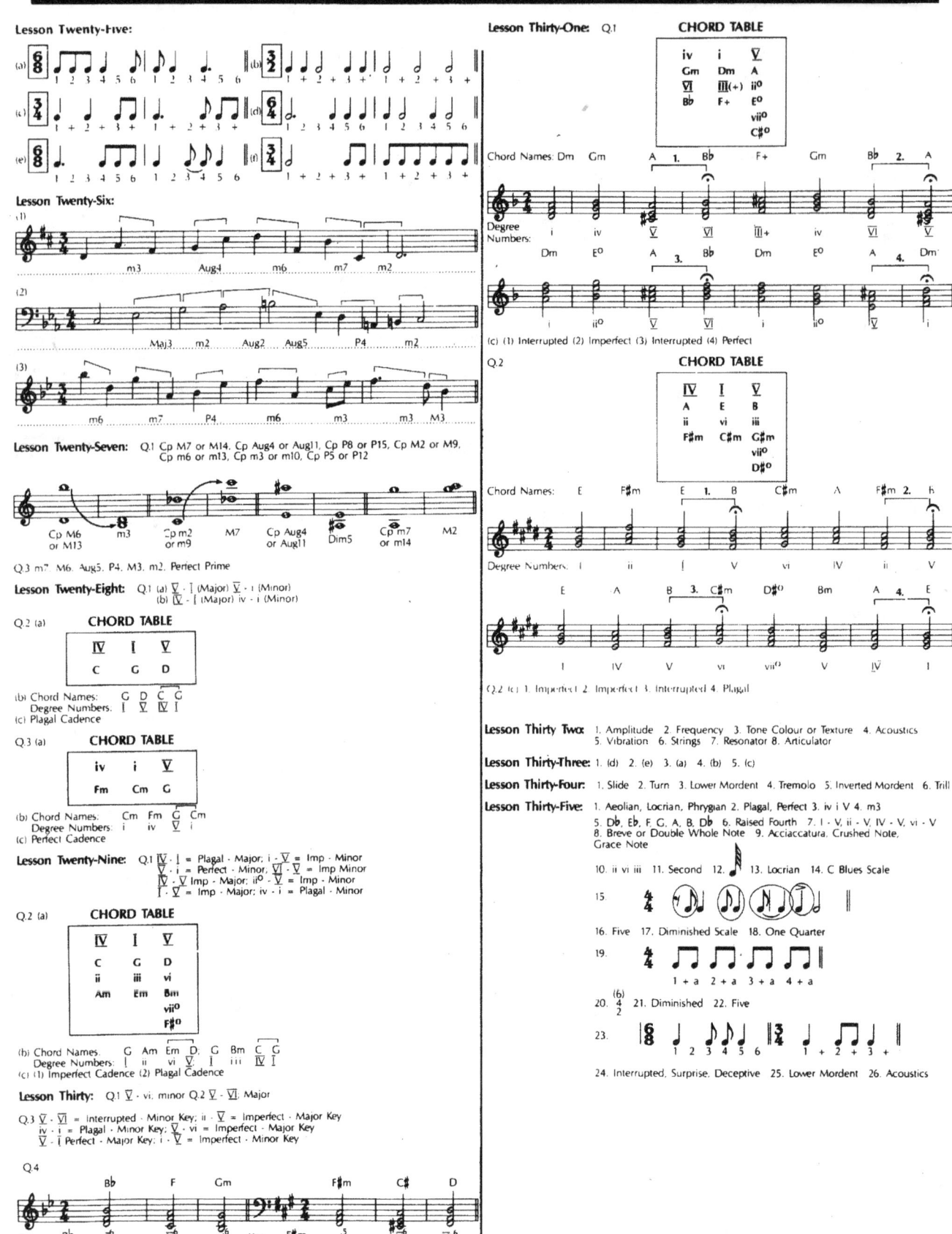

www.ingramcontent.com/pod-product-compliance
Lightning Source LLC
Chambersburg PA
CBHW081524160426

43195CB00015B/2478